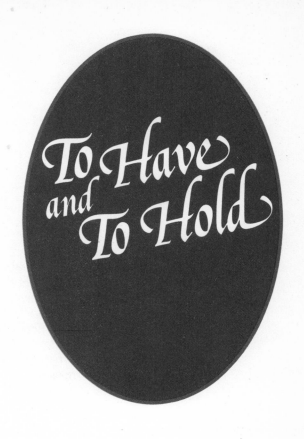

Seminar workshops based on
To Have and to Hold are available.
For further information, contact the
author in care of the publisher.

The exercises and projects used
in this book have been adapted
from *The Compleat Marriage Workbook*
and are used with permission.

Published jointly by
REVIEW AND HERALD® PUBLISHING ASSOCIATION
Hagerstown, MD 21740

PACIFIC PRESS PUBLISHING ASSOCIATION
Boise, ID 83707
Oshawa, Ontario, Canada

To Have and To Hold

A Guide to Successful Marriage

By

Nancy Van Pelt

Dedicated

To Harry,
 my husband,
partner,
friend, and lover,
 with whom I share a happy marriage.

Copyright © 1980 by
Southern Publishing Association
ISBN 0-8280-1026-9 HHES
ISBN 0-8280-1027-7 FHES

Printed in U.S.A.

Acknowledgments

No one ever writes a book "all by oneself," and in my case this is particularly true. *To Have and to Hold* has come to be, not through my ideas alone but because of many other people who gave of their time, talent, and ideas. It results from teaching many family life classes and from counseling couples in all walks of life. It comes as a result of attending classes and talking with pastors and marriage counselors. It is the product of research in a multitude of books written by professionals. It also draws materials from various surveys, including some conducted personally.

Specifically I am indebted to Richard S. Paulson, instructor in speech and English at Reedley College, in Reedley, California, for reading the manuscript and offering editorial and helpful critical evaluations. To Bob Phillips, licensed marriage, family, and child counselor and associate pastor of counseling ministries for the Northwest Baptist Church in Fresno, who provided professional advice and insights on certain aspects of the manuscript. To Paul B. Madsen, MD, also of Fresno, a specialist in obstetrics and gynecology, who provided technical advice for the chapter dealing with sexual fulfillment.

Also to Richard Coffen, my editor, do I owe gratitude for encouragement and editing expertise that helped smooth some of my more outspoken thoughts into soft-spoken ones. To Jo Ann Hobbs, a close friend who spent hours helping me test the validity of many ideas. And to all the "Fulfilled Womanhood" and "Compleat Parent and Marriage" class participants whose experiences have testified that these principles work.

No one can calculate the gratitude family members deserve when an author is writing. My debt goes deep to my husband and children for patience with me when I was preoccupied with writing. My mother, Elsie Reel, also deserves special recognition for supportive help during this time.

And to God be the glory!

Preface

Eight years ago I began teaching a marriage enrichment course for women that I later titled the "Fulfilled Womanhood Seminar." The course created such exciting results that a flame ignited in me to produce my own commonsense guidebook for today's Christian wife.

But something was missing from my idea. The book market became saturated with material for women—*Total Woman, Fascinating Womanhood, You Can Be the Wife of a Happy Husband*—and scores of other how-to books solely for women. Judging by a quick survey of any bookstore, it appeared that the responsibility for a successful marriage rested squarely on the shoulders of the feminine gender, and women attending my classes were quick to point out the injustice of it all!

Was there nothing in print for men? Yes, another section of the bookstore under "Money Management" and "How to Succeed in Business" offered books projecting ideas on how to rise in the business world or how to become the world's next millionaire. But there was next to nothing for the male to read on how to experience success in the marriage relationship.

A new idea was born, and the flame within me burned hotter and brighter to produce a "marriage manual" for wives *and husbands* as well. This book would not only outline a woman's responsibility in holding the marriage together but would also help men find a better balance among the pursual of personal goals, career fulfillment, and a happy family life. It is time for a book that goes beyond theory and preaching to explore hundreds of concrete practical methods in which husband and wife can work together in achieving a happy married life.

Never, in the beginning of my ministry for families, did I imagine where God destined this work to go, because my heart always reached for the individual rather than the masses. Even now, when I speak to a crowded room, I am concerned with the response of each person rather than the group. My experience over the years has taught me that the message in this book is what couples need to hear, comprehend, and act upon in order to discover married happiness. I am not so naive as to believe that one lone book can magically transform *all* marriages. But I firmly believe that marriage need not fail at its present alarming rate. Help is available.

It is my purpose that this book might serve as a guide or textbook in marriage education courses for the church as well as the community. It has been my observation that many such courses explore everything but the dynamics of human relationships, which I consider primary.

The message in this book is directed to three specific groups. The first involves young people who seriously wish to prepare for marriage. I am frequently a guest speaker at high-school family life classes and believe that a fair job is being done in teaching fundamental skills such as money management and the mechanics of establishing a home. But little is being taught regarding interpersonal relationships—how to communicate with, empathize with, and understand the opposite sex. Many problems could be avoided with proper foreknowledge.

Second, I have written this book for Mr. and Mrs. Average Couple, who assume they are doing fairly well on their own since no major problems have surfaced. I hope to open new doors for mediocre marriages so they can experience yet unrecognized possibilities.

Third, this book will help couples caught in the bind of a yet unfulfilled relationship. Perhaps the concepts outlined can serve as a guide to help troubled couples solve their problems and enjoy a plateau of happiness not yet realized.

Creating a meaningful marriage is a complex task that requires knowledge, skill, and effort, as do all worthwhile endeavors. Success awaits the couple who understand what is required of them and consistently work to achieve it. It is my hope that this book, as well as the accompanying classes, will provide the help and support necessary for marital partners who wish to apply themselves seriously to the ongoing effort needed to produce a successful marriage.

Contents

Take any dozen wedded couples, and four will jump overboard; six will stay on deck without joy or love because of children, careers, family, and church; and only two will enjoy a happy marriage.

Chapter at a Glance

For Better or for Worse

Ruth Peale, wife of Dr. Norman Vincent Peale, tells of visiting a university classroom. During her lecture, a beautiful, sophisticated, but scornful young woman in the back of the room challenged, "Mrs. Peale, in your remarks you stated that you thought marriage was the greatest career for a woman. In my opinion, marriage is almost finished, and most of us here feel the same way. We don't think it is necessary or even desirable to link yourself sexually to one partner in your early twenties and limit yourself to that one person for the rest of your life. We think it's ridiculous!"

Every eye was riveted on the coed as she continued. "I am sleeping with a fellow that I like. I don't want to marry him, and I don't think he intends to marry me. This is not my first love affair and probably won't be my last. I can't see anything wrong with this. Someday when and if I choose to have a child, I may be forced by society to marry. But until that time I shall not be a part of it. If I ever do choose to marry and the relationship goes bad, I shall not be trapped in it. Mrs. Peale, we are hardly blind. We see what marriage has done to our par-

---

IV. Marriage—Blessing or Torment: It's Up to You
- A. Three alternatives
    1. Divorce
    2. Standoff
    3. Face the problem

V. Divorce
- A. Socially acceptable today
- B. Why rising divorce rates?
    1. Ease in obtaining a divorce
    2. Decline in family life
    3. Early marriages

    4. Decline in Christian living
- C. Divorce not the answer
    1. Unnecessary
    2. Undesirable

VI. The Ideal Marriage
- A. How to achieve it
- B. Examples of
- C. Influence of

To Have and to Hold

you maintain your present attitudes and code of conduct.''

"I don't see why not," the girl countered defensively, but with less conviction. "Why can't a man-woman relationship be just as meaningful outside of marriage as it is in it?"

"Because," Mrs. Peale responded, "it doesn't have the commitment. It doesn't have the permanence. It doesn't have the depth that comes from total sharing, year after year, working together, knowing you are playing the game for keeps. Do you think we found happiness by waving a magic wand? No! We fought for it and worked for it. To us marriage wasn't a trap—it is a privilege. And there's quite a difference."

As the class stared silently at Mrs. Peale she concluded: "This country is full of good marriages, but they have to be made to happen. It takes brains and determination, and the job is never finished. When you take the time and effort to make a marriage good, the rewards are just enormous.''*

The Compleat Marriage

Many couples fall in love, marry, and assume that the job is completed. They tend to feel that everything else will work out automatically. But hardly anything could be further from the truth. A successful marriage does not come spontaneously or by chance. Instead, a happy marriage—the successful marriage—involves two people working out small difficulties as well as the big ones.

Plato used a ladder to illustrate growth in the marriage relationship. The two upright sides of the ladder stand for the husband and wife, and

ents and to others, and we don't like what we see. Do you have a ready answer?''

Each bright face in the room swung around toward Mrs. Peale, who took a deep breath and replied: "Yes, I have an answer, and I'm living it. I consider myself one of the most fortunate women alive. I am totally married to a man in *every* sense of the word: physically, emotionally, intellectually, spiritually. We're so close that you couldn't put a knife blade between us. We're not two lonely competing individuals. We are one, and nothing else in life can compare to it. But you'll never experience this. You'll never even come within shouting distance of it if

*The Adventure of Being a Wife by Mrs. Norman Vincent Peale, a Fawcett Crest Book (paperback). Copyright © 1971, pages 7-19. Used with permission.

14

The Romance of

and

_____

_____

On our first date we . . . _____

_____

While dating we had the most fun . . . _____

_____

Our favorite song was . . . _____

I was attracted to my mate by . . . _____

_____

Our wedding was . . . _____

_____

_____

On our honeymoon we . . . _____

_____

_____

_____

A keepsake I treasure from the past is . . .

_____

_____

each rung represents something that draws and holds them together in inseparable companionship. The lowest rung is physical attraction, and the highest rung, pure love for God. Each rung of the ladder depends on the other rungs, and thus all become important in order to maintain the unity of the ladder of a compleat marriage.

Someone has defined marriage as "the total commitment of the total person for a total way of life." Such a definition assumes that a couple will work toward goals that they had in mind when they married. To marry for convenience, to escape from a bad home situation, or to give a baby a name is not an adequate goal for a successful marriage. "And they shall be one flesh" (Genesis 2:24) tells, in words as old as the human race, the highest goal in marriage, for marriage is a union of love encompassing all areas of life: physical, emotional, intellectual, and spiritual.

Troubled Marriages Need Professional Help

Many Christian couples feel reluctant to seek counsel or even to admit that their marriage has reached the point of needing help, because they assume that marital problems are incompatible with a vital spiritual life. They feel that they have failed spiritually if they must admit to trouble within the home. But if a couple gets immediate help for a troubled marriage, they will avoid much unnecessary pain.

Sixty percent of those who encounter marital tensions turn first to the pastor for help, yet somehow they often hold back from baring their most intimate problems. They may fear that experiences shared in strictest confidence may leak to other church members or end up as illustrations in sermons. And far too often well-meaning but poorly trained pastors revert to clichés such as "pray about it."

Thus, on the one hand the churches must be more responsible to the needs of their members by recognizing the existence of family problems and by presenting continuing educational programs for all age groups. Church leaders need more awareness of the tensions arising within marriages and should educate themselves so that they can offer definite and intelligent help.

On the other hand those seeking answers must remember that most

Drawing by Chon Day, © 1944, 1972, The New Yorker Magazine, Inc.

problems have no instant cures—that even the best clergyman or counselor can basically only offer support and compassion. In cases where a mate refuses to see a counselor or get help, the other partner should seek help alone. Surely the Lord smiles on those who search for new ways to improve family relationships, because the Christian life involves continual growth and improvement in all aspects.

Most couples need to develop more adequate interpersonal relationships and communication skills, but Christ's influence in the life is the important key to a meaningful marriage. Without a Christ-centered relationship, a couple can find periods of contentment and morsels of happiness, but the union remains just human, and therefore, mediocre.

Our needs as human beings can never be fully realized until we are rightly related not only to ourselves and to our fellowmen but also to God.

Some people seem concerned about satisfying only the animal instincts of food, shelter, clothing, and sex, but becoming restless, bored, or despondent, they fail to function as God service the archbishop asked a nervous little girl what *matrimony* was. "Oh," she said, "it is a state of terrible torment that those who enter are compelled to undergo for a time in order to fit them for a better world."

The local priest interrupted the little girl: "No! No! You're thinking of *purgatory*."

"Let her alone," said the old archbishop, smiling. "What do you or I know about it?"

Whether marriage becomes a blessing or a torment depends on the couple involved.

A twenty-nine-year-old woman sat across from me and told me that if I could not drastically change her husband within the next few weeks, she would have to divorce him. (I was supposed to accomplish this in spite of his refusal to accept counseling.) I listed for her the alternatives, which are the same for all unhappily married partners. Whether the problems are trivial or severe, each spouse has only three choices.

The first alternative is divorce—the great American cop-out. Many parties today determine that they have real provocation for divorce, and they obtain one—deciding to be more careful the next time. Far too many counselors, even so-called "Christian" counselors, advise divorce. Too often, however, divorce is an escape mechanism and is thus the most immature of the three choices.

The second alternative is to endure a standoff relationship—tough it out, grin and bear it, wear a mask. All this goes on without working to improve the unfortunate situation. The world will never know how terrible things are at home unless one of the spouses squeals; so the two playact in front of others and silently endure a rotten relationship. Millions of married couples

designed them to. Innate within each one of us is the need for a personal relationship with God. Spirituality is the missing ingredient in our age of permissiveness. As a couple commit themselves and their home to a higher power, they become bound together as partners in a stable, successful marriage relationship.

A State of Torment

A Catholic archbishop visited a mining district one day to confirm a class about to join the church. During the

Evaluate Your Marriage

Many of us try to build a marriage with no specific objective or goal in mind. God has a plan and a purpose for us to fulfill in marriage. If we lose sight of the goal, then we will concentrate only on our motions. This might be similar to the pilot who announced to his passengers, "We're lost, folks. But cheer up; we're making excellent headway."

The Bible urges, "Examine yourselves" (2 Corinthians 13:5) and, "Let each one test [examine] his own work" (Galatians 6:4, RSV). The Christian home builder needs to seek ways to improve and increase the happiness of his/her mate. Some couples experience a mediocre marriage because they haven't *planned* for a better one.

Fill out this marriage evaluation independently of your mate, then compare the results to see whether you are in agreement. If you are, you can decide on united action. If you disagree, you can explore ways to come closer together.

1. How would you describe your marriage? (Be specific.)

2. How do you think your mate would describe your marriage? (Be specific.)

3. List the strong points in your marriage.

4. List the weak areas in your marriage.

5. I am happiest in our marriage when . . .

6. We are happiest in our marriage when . . .

7. In my marriage I hurt most when . . .

8. My mate and I differ about the following things:

9. When we have had difficulty in the past, the following things have helped make it better:

10. List some changes that you need strength from God to make in your home.

have chosen this alternative because it is easier than having to face certain personal deficiencies and then doing something about them—another immature decision.

The third alternative involves facing personal problems and making an intelligent choice to build a happy marriage out of the existing one. Even those with "incompatible personalities" can learn to work out personal deficiencies. The word *incompatible* is too frequently used by people who are too lazy to work out their own hang-ups, so they run away by divorcing and remarrying. Numerous studies have shown that when couples with neurotic marriage relationships divorce—no matter how good their intentions are—they nearly always remarry into the very same type of neurotic relationship.

One psychiatrist in reporting his track record observed that in all cases where *both* marriage partners had come to him for at least four sessions together (even if they had already filed for divorce), not a single couple ended up getting a divorce. Not only have these couples not divorced, but also in every case—once they got over the hurdle of deciding to make the best of their present marriage—they have made significant improvements in their

marital and other interpersonal relationships. Facing personal hang-ups is not easy, but it is by far the most mature of the three alternatives.

"There are no unhappy marriages, only marriage partners who are immature," says Dr. David Mace, renowned marriage counselor. If partners could develop more mature attitudes, all areas of their relationship would improve. Indeed, the journey toward the ideal marriage is the journey from childishness to personal maturity.

Something Worse

Today people tend to accept divorce as socially acceptable. The latest statistics reveal that 38 percent of all first marriages end in divorce, and the church is not immune from such statistics. Divorce in Los Angeles County has hit the 50 percent mark. Affluent Marin County in California leads the nation with a whopping 70 percent of all marriages ending in divorce. Statistics also tell us that a second marriage is almost twice as likely to fail as a first marriage.

Several factors contribute to the increased divorce rate in recent years. Easy do-it-yourself divorces constitute one reason. An ad from one local paper reads: "Divorce, only $70. It costs noth-

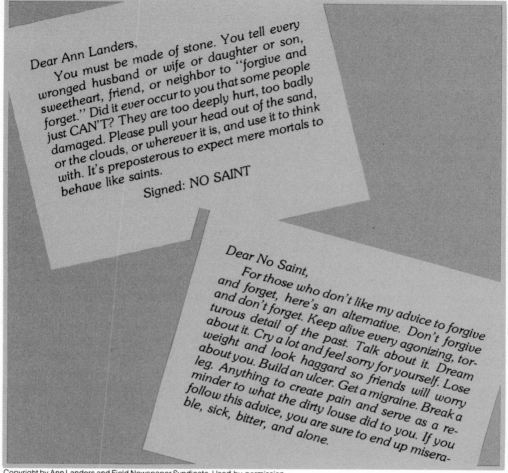

Dear Ann Landers,
You must be made of stone. You tell every wronged husband or wife or daughter or son, sweetheart, friend, or neighbor to "forgive and forget." Did it ever occur to you that some people just CAN'T? They are too deeply hurt, too badly damaged. Please pull your head out of the sand, or the clouds, or wherever it is, and use it to think with. It's preposterous to expect mere mortals to behave like saints.
Signed: NO SAINT

Dear No Saint,
For those who don't like my advice to forgive and forget, here's an alternative. Don't forgive and don't forget. Keep alive every agonizing, torturous detail of the past. Talk about it. Dream about it. Cry a lot and feel sorry for yourself. Lose weight and look haggard so friends will worry about you. Build an ulcer. Get a migraine. Break a leg. Anything to create pain and serve as a reminder to what the dirty louse did to you. If you follow this advice, you are sure to end up miserable, sick, bitter, and alone.

ing to dial our toll-free number."

Another contributing factor is a decline in family life. A few years ago the home formed the mainstream of activity, but now it serves more as a launching pad, where family members stop in briefly to refuel before moving on to other areas.

Early marriages and a lack of preparation and training for marriage can also contribute to the increasing divorce rate. Marriage seems so natural that we usually assume one can succeed as a marriage partner without special education. The fact is people are not born with the knowledge and understanding necessary to work out the complexities of marriage.

A decline in positive Christian living has also influenced the divorce rate. Many people try to live as if there are no principles or truths to follow. Doubts, frustrations, and despair saturate their minds, and they turn to kinky substitutes in a vain attempt to find meaning in life. Drugs, sex, the occult, form much of the restless activity that they pursue in a frantic effort to keep one step ahead of emptiness and loneliness.

In most cases divorce solves little and evades much. It leaves in its path heartache, loneliness, and a feeling of personal failure. If it is a cure for a sick marriage, then the cure often turns out to be worse than the sickness.

Block the idea of divorce from your mind, and never use it as a threat against your partner. It may be the last thing you really want, but your pride may not allow you to back down from words spoken in haste.

One eminent marriage counselor notes that most divorces are not only unnecessary but also undesirable. In most cases both husband and wife are worse off after terminating their relationship than before. Those contemplating divorce fail to take into account the serious readjustments it necessitates. Since many divorcées find such readjustment depressing, their rates of insanity, suicide, and death are two to three times higher than those for married persons of the same ages.

Something Better

However, the man and woman who enter marriage with the idea of making it a "total commitment of the total person for a total way of life" can look forward to a gratifying marriage. Barring the insane, neurotic, or alcoholic person, who should avoid marriage anyway, almost anyone with a certain amount of com-

mon sense, maturity, and effort can attain a reasonably successful marriage.

A friend said not long ago, "I'm in my mid-thirties and have met only one happily married couple in my life." She didn't need logical arguments to convince her of happy marriages. She needed living examples in vivid color—flesh-and-blood people who live in harmony and radiate marital happiness and optimism.

Perhaps you are saying, "What on earth can we do about this? We are just one couple in a fast-moving impersonal world." But you are not so insignificant as to have no influence. You can make a unique and important contribution within your circle of friends. The important question here is not whether the institution of marriage will survive, but will your marriage survive? When your marriage is happy, you will have a direct bearing on friends as well as on the eventual marriage of your own children. Someone has estimated that each married couple directly influences twelve other couples a year. If this ratio could be maintained, the world could be changed!

Your marriage can be more than just an influence. It can also inspire others. Since happy marriages seem to be on the endangered species list, you'd probably create a new sensation in your neighborhood.

My husband, Harry, was attending an in-service training conference at his hospital facility and found himself teamed with an attractive female divorcée. As part of the conference, the pairs were to interview each other and report to the group interesting facts. Her report centered on how she envied Harry's close family life.

As one Christian has written, "One well-ordered, well-disciplined family tells more in behalf of Christianity than all the sermons that can be preached."

The Forgiveness Board

In pencil write out on the board below what it is you are having trouble forgiving your mate for. After praying about it, ask God to help you forgive and forget. Then erase it from the board. Let this symbolize that you can forget it with God's help.

"Let all bitterness, and wrath, and anger, and clamour, and evil speaking, be put away from you, with all malice: and be ye kind one to another, tenderhearted, forgiving one another, even as God for Christ's sake hath forgiven you" (Ephesians 4:31, 32).

Further reading you will enjoy...

Bietz, Reinhold. *HAPPINESS UNDER ONE ROOF.*
Mace, David and Vera. *HOW TO HAVE A HAPPY MARRIAGE.*
Vandeman, George E. *HAPPINESS WALL TO WALL.*

*It has been said: "The cure for all the ills
and wrongs, the cares, the sorrow and the
crimes of humanity, all lies in one word: 'love.'
It is the divine vitality that everywhere produces
and restores life. To each and every one of us,
it gives the power of working miracles if we
will."*

Chapter at a Glance

I. Love
A. A woman's whole existence
   1. The female capacity for love
   2. Her need for daily expressions of romantic love
      a. The key to her self-worth
      b. Her satisfaction with marital life
      c. Her sexual responsiveness
   3. Many men unaware of female needs
   4. Emotional security ultimate female goal
   5. Seeks constant reassurance of this
B. A man's love is different
   1. The male approach to love is—
      a. less tied to the emotions
      b. more practical in nature
      c. more calm and rational
   2. His love is demonstrated
      a. by his support of the family

Love Your Mate

From the crib to the grave we all reach out for someone to love us and for someone we can love. Indeed, love is necessary for survival. Without it we lose the will to live; our mental and physical vitality lessens; resistance lowers; and fatal illnesses can result. When we experience love, we glow with a radiance that affects us physically, mentally, socially, and spiritually.

For the lack of love thousands commit suicide each year. Another multitude flock to the divorce courts to free themselves so that they can begin their search for love again. Mental hospitals hold many who, for the want of human affection, have slipped beyond the reach of sanity. Battered and neglected children suffer marked signs of neurosis or psychosis. Research has shown that infants who lack a close, affectionate relationship with their mothers not only reveal signs of emotional disturbances but are physically dwarfed as well. Within the homes for senior citizens sit thousands of aged fathers and mothers—unnoticed, unloved, and dying a tear at a time for want of affection.

Dr. Smiley Blanton, in his book,

    b. through protective behavior
3. The male nature is
    a. kind, affectionate
    b. loving, sentimental
4. The male nature different from the female's in loving
    a. Cannot live without love
    b. Love a motivation for him to work, plan, sacrifice, invest, expand, and pursue

B. Definition
    1. Involves a commitment
    2. Is unconditional
    3. Attempts to meet the needs of others
    4. Enables us to love ourselves
    5. Allows the other to be himself
    6. Is permanent

II. Genuine Love
    A. A principle put into action

Love or Perish, says, "For more than forty years I have sat in my office and listened while people of all ages and classes told me of their hopes and fears. . . . As I look back over the long, full years, one truth emerges clearly in my mind—the universal need for love. . . . They cannot survive without love: they must have it or they will perish."

When love fails, marriages fall into ruins and impossible frustrations deluge those involved and those around them. Such emotional pressure results in juvenile delinquency, adult crime, alcoholism, and various forms of drug addiction. Finally, the attempt to destroy oneself may end this ruinous cycle. As Dante observed, "It is love that spins the universe, and when we fail to use love properly, all of life suffers."

The truth is, we all crave love in huge quantities, and sometimes it seems that we can never get enough. Love is, in fact, the single most important force contributing to our total well-being. Impelled by its motivating power, we can forge ahead through life's bitterest moments and withstand insults and cruelty.

We must be realistic about such wishes, however, for it is unlikely that we will ever be loved as completely as we might wish to be. Anyone expecting unqualified love all the time expects more than is humanly possible from another person. Furthermore, it is only realistic to recognize that—right or wrong—society demands a certain standard of performance before it deems us lovable or even acceptable.

Love— a Woman's Whole Existence

Love is necessary for all human survival, and it seems that females have a great capacity for love—both to give and to receive it. For example, a woman's great capacity to love surfaces when she picks up needle and thread to mend the tear in a shirt. When she prepares a meal, her love mingles with the food. When she rises for the two o'clock feeding, she does so with love. When she dresses the baby, love is the crowning drive. When she frosts a birthday cake, love shines through. When she feeds a stray kitten at the back door, she has tapped her love resource. When she gazes romantically into the glow of a warm fireplace, it symbolizes her love.

A woman's capacity to love can draw the very best from a man—so in-

Getting a Few Thoughts Together

> "For this is the message that ye heard from the beginning, that we should love one another" (1 John 3:11).

1. What makes me feel loved?

2. What makes my partner feel loved?

3. Name some new ways that you can express love to your partner through actions this week.

4. Name some new ways that you can express love to your partner through words this week.

spiring him that he may lay aside a life of crime. Her love can spark hope and renewed trust in a man—even making him feel wanted, worthwhile, important, and almost great. The wave of her hand as he leaves in the morning and her warm greeting when he arrives home at night evidence her love. When his nerves are shattered and signs of exhaustion surface, her love can comfort him. When discouragement crushes him and his hopes and dreams have crumbled, she can help him build new ones.

The world needs the gentle, loving, affectionate touch of a woman, and the love within her merely awaits the right man to tap its fountain of warmth and affection. But women also have a great capacity for love. Not only are they capable of sharing vast amounts of affection, but they also have a large capacity to absorb love in return. As Lord Byron put it in *Don Juan:* "Man's love is of man's life a thing apart, 'Tis a woman's whole existence" (I, 194). And the key to her own storehouse of love lies within the hands of the man who offers to her marital happiness and emotional security by returning that deep affection.

Often before marriage, when a young man woos a young woman, he persists night and day with loving words and tender deeds. But once he has won her as his bride, he often fails to recognize her intense need to feel loved on a day-to-day basis for the rest of her life.

Because of her capacity for affection, daily expressions of romantic love are vital to a woman's existence. It is the key to her self-worth, her satisfaction with married life, and her sexual responsiveness. If a man feels trapped in a bored, tired marriage, he might look to himself for part of the answer. By consistently and thoughtfully expressing romantic love, many men could melt even the most frigid wife.

One bewildered husband complained of not being able to understand his wife. "I have given her everything she wants and needs. We have a custom-built home in the best section of town, microwave oven, color TV, and the whole bit. I'm a faithful husband who doesn't drink or beat the kids. But she says she's miserable, and I can't figure out why!" This man didn't realize that his wife would trade the custom-built house and all its conveniences for a few affectionate words from him. Microwave ovens and color televisions do not make a woman feel cherished, but being somebody's sweetheart does.

Many men are nearly totally unaware of a woman's need for romantic love, because for centuries society has focused on women meeting the sexual needs of their husbands. It might even be that some men would settle for a business arrangement of sorts in marriage as long as it included meals, housekeeping, hostessing, and sexual privileges as the occasion called for them. Romance might be an added benefit, but certainly not a requirement.

Not so with a woman! Such a relationship would drive her wild with frustration. She must have something more meaningful. She yearns to be someone special to her husband—to be cherished, respected, appreciated, and loved. Only recently has it surfaced that a woman's needs for emotional fulfillment is *every bit* as pressing as is the male's need for sexual release. It is as unjustifiable for a man to ignore his wife's need for romantic love as it is for her to deny him his sexual urges.

This explains why a homemaker spends so much time thinking about her husband during the day, why an anniversary is more important to her than it is to him, and why she feels so frustrated when her husband forgets such courtesies. It also explains why a woman constantly "reaches" for her husband when at the end of the day he gets home and settles comfortably behind the newspaper or in front of the television.

Emotional security is the ultimate goal in a woman's life. Therefore, many a woman continually seeks reassurance from her husband by asking him to do something for her that she could *easily* do for herself. His willingness serves as a measure of his love and regard.

Sometimes a woman expects her husband to do what she wants done *without being asked,* because she sees

"My husband and lover."

31

occur in the bedroom as a result of such female behavior. He makes sexual advances, and she withdraws. In an effort to be considerate of her wishes, he turns over and tries to sleep. At this point, she might cry or nurse hurt and angry feelings. Why? She assumes that she should be so irresistibly attractive that her husband will persist in his efforts despite all the obstacles she puts in his way. If he doesn't insist, she concludes that he doesn't love her enough, and her emotional security becomes threatened.

Such game-playing causes tremendous confusion. Women should learn how to verbalize their needs in an open and honest way. And men must recognize the enormous need on the part of women for security.

Some men feel, "If I told my wife every day that I love her, it wouldn't mean anything anymore." However, loving words spoken sincerely to a wife will always mean something special. If she responds with enthusiasm, you will know instantly that you hit your mark. But some women do not say much or give any visible indication that they heard or understood the words. This doesn't mean the loving expressions weren't needed, however. Some women have been conditioned to hold in their feelings and only seldom respond with an outward display of affection. But such messages will work in her heart. Give her time.

Perhaps your wife knows very well that you appreciate and care for her, but she still needs to hear those words of endearment. I saved one letter from the dozens Harry wrote me during our engagement when miles separated us. Over and over again he wrote, "I love you, I love you, I love you." The words appeared on the front of the letter, the back, and the envelope. I have never tired of reading those words.

this as an evidence of even a greater degree of love for her. Consequently, she may not always tell him what she really wants done. And if he fails to do what she desires, she becomes indignant.

This female phenomenon often shows up in our home. I am very capable and self-sufficient, but I will often draw the line at such a small task as filling the gas tank in the car. It has nothing to do with male-female role. Instead it is linked to my need for emotional security. If Harry assumes this responsibility, he has reassured me of my place in his affections.

At times this can go even one step further. Sometimes a wife may deny that she wants what she actually does want. If her husband takes her at her word, she feels disturbed. She rationalizes that she is so important to her husband that he should understand and meet her desires, regardless. For example, misunderstandings often

One caution for wives: Some women expect too much attention from their husbands. The mass media—novels, movies, magazines, and television soap operas—have often portrayed a distorted picture of the harsh realities involved in marriage. If the wife compares her husband to the professionally groomed hero on the screen, the husband may most likely fall short. Feelings of frustration, unhappiness, and bitterness can then result. Some women tend to live in a dream world and imagine that one can live on love alone. Although romance is sweet and good, a cake made from nothing but sugar would soon dissolve.

A Man's Love Is Different

Men are lovers, but their approach to love differs from that of women's. Men are affectionate by nature, and it is a gross misunderstanding to intimate that men resort to affection only when it brings them sexual rewards. Although man's love may not be so directly tied to his emotions as is a woman's, it is still

"If I had the gift of being able to speak in other languages without learning them, and could speak in every language there is in all of heaven and earth, but didn't love others, I would only be making noise. If I had the gift of prophecy and knew all about what is going to happen in the future, knew everything about 'everything,' but didn't love others, what good would it do? Even if I had the gift of faith so that I could speak to a mountain and make it move, I would still be worth nothing at all without love. If I gave everything I have to poor people, and if I were burned alive for preaching the Gospel but didn't love others, it would be of no value whatever.

"Love is very patient and kind, never jealous or envious, never boastful or proud, never haughty or selfish or rude. Love does not demand its own way. It is not irritable or touchy. It does not hold grudges and will hardly even notice when others do it wrong. It is never glad about injustice, but rejoices whenever truth wins out. If you love someone you will be loyal to him no matter what the cost. You will always believe in him, always expect the best of him, and always stand your ground in defending him.

"All the special gifts and powers from God will someday come to an end, but love goes on forever" (1 Corinthians 13:1-8, TLB*).

* From Taylor. The Living Bible, Paraphrased (Wheaton: Tyndale House, 1971). Used by permission.

very real. He is just more often practical and less romantic in his demonstrations of love.

After a young man pops the question, he may immediately begin talking to his bride-to-be about their financial future, which he considers as much an evidence of his love as his kisses. A father who rolls on the floor while tickling his daughter into gales of laughter demonstrates a daddy's love for his daughter. A husband shows his love as he juggles the bank account to purchase a dishwasher for the home, a pair of shoes for Bobby, or a new robe for his wife. The man who invests in an acreage is planning for the future with the ones he loves. A woman might regard these as necessities, but they show the man's desire to give and share and provide. This, too, is love.

Thus, although few men possess the ability to sweep a woman off her feet, they demonstrate their love in calm and rational lines. For example, a husband brings home paychecks regularly— converting his entire earnings to the needs of the family. A man may feel very little emotion in rising at 6:30 five mornings a week and working around the clock, but his basic reason for persevering is his love for his family. Men endure this routine for a lifetime and often ask for little more than meals and an embrace at the proper time.

When a man opens the car door for his wife, assists her in and out, and takes her arm as they walk, he reveals his protective instincts over her. He wants to shield her from danger or anything that might threaten her, which is another element of male love.

No matter how rough the exterior of a man, tenderness and love still lurk underneath the surface. While I taught in a rural community, a wife told me how her husband, a wheat farmer, would plow around a bird's nest so as not to disturb the nest or eggs. A man is by nature kind, affectionate, loving, and sentimental. He has tender ways and can be deeply thoughtful. And he expresses his love for his family in a multitude of ways.

Whereas love does not make up a man's entire existence, he cannot live without it. Love motivates a man to work, plan, sacrifice, invest, expand, and pursue. It is for love that he gives up his singleness, signs on the dotted line, accepts full financial responsibility for her and all children born to the union, and gives away his most prized possession—freedom.

Rewrite the apostle Paul's beautiful description of love as it is given in The Living Bible.* Use your own name in the blanks.

"_____ is very patient and kind, never jealous or envious, never boastful or proud, never haughty or selfish or rude. _____ does not demand . . . [his/her] own way. _____ is not irritable or touchy. _____ does not hold grudges and will hardly even notice when others do . . [him/her] wrong. _____ is never glad about injustice, but rejoices whenever truth wins out."

Now rewrite the rest of the passage, using your mate's name in the blanks.

"If you love _____ you will be loyal to him [or her] no matter what the cost. You will always believe in _____, always expect the best of _____, and always stand your ground in defending _____" (1 Corinthians 13:4-7).

---

*From Taylor. The Living Bible, Paraphrased (Wheaton: Tyndale House, 1971). Used by permission.

There is no limit to the love a woman can receive from a man when she learns to open the door to his heart, for she can provide the right emotional atmosphere for him to freely expose his feelings and dare to share his love.

Genuine Love

We have emphasized that romance is a needed commodity in marriages today, but love means far more than just the feelings expressed in romantic affection, as important as they are. Dr. Karl Menninger, a great Christian psychiatrist, expressed it this way: "We do not fall into love; rather we grow into love." Love in marriage matures as a couple applies the principle of love in everyday life. Genuine love, then, goes beyond the feelings of love and becomes a principle that must be put into action. We must not only expect to be treated with love and consideration, but we must also *act* with love and consideration.

Yet it is very difficult for most of us to consistently express our love day in and day out. Few of us *feel* like being tender, thoughtful, considerate, and helpful every day of our lives, because our feelings are easily altered by moods, foods eaten, the weather, illness, the reaction of our mates toward us, and a host of other variables. Since feelings are unstable, those who contend that love is primarily a feeling will make unstable lovers. They will proceed through life indulging in what feels good and pursuing "that old feeling" immortalized in song.

Of course feelings constitute a component of love. Love wouldn't be very interesting or much fun if we didn't have "that feeling." Indeed, the first attraction between individuals rests primarily on feelings, and a love relationship will hardly ensue unless love feelings surface.

However, in marriage some of the early feelings of young love dwindle. No one can constantly live at an emotionally feverish high. When these first feelings diminish, moments will come when emotional satisfaction in the relationship seems relatively low. Negative feelings may poison the atmosphere. At these times we must exercise the principle of acting love. With the passing of time and by exercising the principles of love, young love can mature into a more genuine love that binds hearts and lives together—counteracting negative feelings.

The Principles of Genuine Love

Genuine love involves a commitment. Since it would be too demanding to enter a total personal commitment with several people of the opposite sex, we eventually must narrow our choice to one person. Most people do not have the emotional energy to maintain several love relationships concurrently. It is too exhausting.

Immature and inexperienced persons often enter personal commitments that they later find impossible to honor. Moonlight, music, and romance go to their heads, and they make a promise of love that they later find themselves unable to live with. Such people abandon the commitment made, head for the courts, and proceed recklessly toward a new love relationship without ever challenging their personal ingenuity, developing their resources, or testing their coping abilities. Love will work if we work at it, but people today fail to work at giving love a chance, and wise individuals select carefully before investing such a sacred commodity in a lifelong commitment.

Genuine love is unconditional. A love with conditions attached isn't genuine, and only in an atmosphere of unconditional love can we lower our defenses enough for intimacy to develop.

A certain housewife who sensed conditional love from her husband told how his love seemed to be based on whether the house was clean and orderly at all times. She said that she needed to know he loved her whether the house was clean or not in order to keep the house clean! Similarly, a woman may sometimes give sexual love based on conditions to which her husband must measure up. Such a wife promises to gratify her husband's sexual needs provided that he completes tasks beforehand or that he meets certain standards of behavior.

Perfect demonstrations of unconditional love are not consistent with human behavior. Our emotional and psychological weaknesses prevent us from being totally free to give love unconditionally to others. But unconditional love provides an ideal toward which we may strive.

Genuine love attempts to meet the needs of the other. A favorite cartoon of mine shows Charlie Brown in his pajamas on his way to Snoopy's doghouse with a glass of water. The caption reads: "Love is getting someone a glass of water in the middle of the night."

It rarely taps our energies to be loving when our mates are affectionate and considerate. But how difficult it is to be loving under more trying circumstances—when he speaks unkindly, when she refuses to listen, when he is late for meals, when she neglects the mending.

In the face of such problems, I have developed what I call "the test of love." A person is to respond in a loving manner even though the mate has acted thoughtlessly. When we can dedicate ourselves to fulfilling the needs of the other even though our own needs have been thwarted, we are exercising genuine love.

Test Your Lovingness

Take this short test and compare your love and the love of your mate with the Biblical definition of love. Consider your everyday interactions with one another. When you have completed this exercise, share your responses with your mate.

LOVE . . .		No Problem at All	Pretty Good	So-So	Need Help Badly
is slow to lose patience (doesn't demonstrate irritations)	Me				
	Mate				
looks for a way of being constructive (contributes to the other's needs or life)	Me				
	Mate				
is not possessive (allows freedom to express individuality)	Me				
	Mate				
is neither anxious to impress (does not show itself off)	Me				
	Mate				
nor does it cherish inflated ideas of its own importance (not self-centered or conceited)	Me				
	Mate				
has good manners (demonstrates discretion and decency)	Me				
	Mate				
does not pursue selfish advantage (major concern is for the needs of others)	Me				
	Mate				
is not touchy (not hypersensitive or easily hurt)	Me				
	Mate				
does not keep account of evil (forgets wrongs that have been forgiven)	Me				
	Mate				
does not . . . gloat over the wickedness of other people (doesn't excuse own sins because of other's sins)	Me				
	Mate				
shares the joy of those who live by the truth (active fellowship with dedicated Christians)	Me				
	Mate				
knows no limit to its endurance (overlooks faults and endures hardships)	Me				
	Mate				
knows . . . no end to its trust (expresses faith and believes the best)	Me				
	Mate				
knows . . . no fading of its hope (not fickle or negative)	Me				
	Mate				
can outlast anything (endures all obstacles)	Me				
	Mate				

Genuine love enables us to love ourselves. Genuine love of another is premised on a genuine love for oneself. The Bible asks us to love our neighbors *as ourselves.* The implication is clear: Whatever we would do for our neighbor, we should also do for ourselves. In the marriage relationship this means that we will do for our mates what we do also for ourselves.

Christians often find this concept difficult to grasp, because much of the Christian doctrine revolves around "doing for others." We have regarded thinking of "self" or feeling worthy as inherently sinful. But loving oneself does not involve pride or a noisy conceit. Instead it is a quiet sense of security blessed by feelings of adequacy. When a person possesses such self-respect, he appreciates his own worth. He is able, in a healthy way, to assess his abilities in a realistic manner and feels assured that he is equal to others. Pride, however, involves an unrealistic appraisal that leads one to feel superior to others.

The thought of appreciating ourselves or feeling worthwhile is often a foreign thought, yet marriage partners can engage in satisfying relationships only in proportion to the respect and belief they hold for themselves.

Genuine love allows the other to be himself. Love is not possessive (1 Corinthians 13:4). Genuine love, then, affirms the uniqueness of the individual by the marriage partners giving their mates a freedom to be themselves. It does not attempt to possess or manipulate others. It means that we will preserve our mate's freedom to think his own thoughts, retain his own feelings, and make his own decisions. It releases others to become their best selves according to how *they* perceive the picture.

Such a love leaves room for others to have a variety of friends and interests beyond the marriage relationship, for we each need a certain amount of "space" in which to develop our identities and potentialities. By not attempting to become the other's entire life, we free him or her to enjoy the full range of life's wondrous experiences.

Genuine love is permanent. One of the most beautiful characteristics listed in 1 Corinthians 13:8 is the permanence of genuine love. Love never fails. Yet the divorce courts are jammed with bitter and disillusioned couples, all of whom at one point or another claimed to be in love.

Much of what we call love today begins with ardent passion, but like a beautiful plant, it will wither and die if the parties involved do not understand how to nourish and care for it. Love, even genuine love, is fragile.

It takes self-discipline to be a genuinely loving person. In the first chapter I quoted my favorite definition of marriage: "the total commitment of the total person for a total life." The key word is *commitment,* which in turn implies permanence.

In our marriage it operates like this. The feelings and circumstances of the moment cannot alter the love that Harry and I have for each other. Our commitment to one another holds us permanently together even though our emotions may fluctuate. At times Harry fails me, and my romantic feelings die. On other occasions I seriously falter in my efforts to be a genuinely loving mate. Sometimes we find ourselves consumed with feelings of anger, resentment, bitterness, and despair. But we have pledged ourselves to one another in an uncompromising decision when we echoed the words: "In sickness and in health, . . . for richer for poorer, . . . for better or for worse, . . . from this day forward . . ." Our romantic feelings may fail us, but our genuine love holds us together through those troubled times.

The key to putting the principle of genuine love into practice is *selflessness*. Fulfillment in a total love relationship comes as one matures out of self-centeredness into genuine love. The way to receive love is to give it. Jesus said, "Give, and it shall be given unto you" (Luke 6:38), and the teaching He enunciates applies equally to the area of marriage. If you want a deeper love relationship, begin by giving more love. Instead of waiting for your mate to demonstrate affection for you, take it upon yourself to initiate the first actions. Discover your mate's needs, and begin to fill them *now!*

Further reading you will enjoy...

Benson, Dan. *THE TOTAL MAN*, Chapter 11.
Dobson, James. *WHAT WIVES WISH THEIR HUSBANDS KNEW ABOUT WOMEN*, Chapter 5.
Mallory, James. *THE KINK AND I*, Chapter 6.
Mayhall, Jack. *MARRIAGE TAKES MORE THAN LOVE*, chapters 18-23.
Mow, Anna. *THE SECRET OF MARRIED LOVE*.
Powell, John. *THE SECRET OF STAYING IN LOVE*, chapters 1 and 2.
Williams, Page. *DO YOURSELF A FAVOR: LOVE YOUR WIFE*.

"God grant me the serenity to accept the things
I cannot change, the courage to change the
things I can, and the wisdom to know
the difference."

Chapter at a Glance

I. Acceptance

A. What acceptance involves
1. Viewing your mate as a person of worth
2. Liking your mate as he/she is
3. Respecting his/her right to be dissimilar from you
4. Allowing him/her to possess own feelings about matters
5. Accepting his/her attitudes, no matter how different

B. Acceptance does not mean—
1. you pretend your mate is perfect
2. no faults exist

C. Acceptance means—
1. recognizing imperfections
2. recognizing that areas need changing
3. accepting the total person

II. Unacceptance

A. Common forms of unacceptance
1. Criticism
2. Belittling remarks
3. Subtle suggestions
4. Tiny hints

Accept Your Mate

During our engagement I remember insisting over and over again that Harry was *the* perfect man, but soon the intimacy of marriage revealed faults and habits in my "perfect" mate that irritated me. I decided married life would be more enjoyable if he would conform to my ideas of how a perfect mate should order his life. It was almost as if an unseen force compelled me to "help" him overcome his deficiencies and become more acceptable to me, my family, and others. This pattern continued for a number of years without success.

A great deal of marital discord arises when one partner sets about trying to change the other, for it is basic to our happiness to feel respected, liked, and accepted as we are. We feel uncomfortable when under pressure to change our habits, personality, or preferences. Especially at home it is imperative that we learn to accept differences, tolerate idiosyncrasies, and respect individuality.

What Is Acceptance?

What does it mean to accept your mate? It means that you view your mate as a person of worth. It means that you

---

5. Nonverbal attitudes
6. Nagging

B. The results of nagging
   1. Increases problems
   2. Kills love
   3. Arouses defenses
   4. Doesn't work

III. Attempts to Change
A. The reasons behind attempts to change another
B. How to point out mistakes—if you must
C. How to change your mate

IV. Developing Acceptance
A. The steps to acceptance
   1. recognize a self-righteous attitude
   2. Allow mate freedom to be himself/herself
   3. Concentrate on good points
   4. Express acceptance in words
B. How to express acceptance in words
   1. Express appreciation for personality and character
   2. Mention specific areas where hopes are being fulfilled

"Suppose he doesn't get the best marks in his class. Do you get the highest salary in your office?"

Drawing by Hoff, © 1950, 1978, The New Yorker Magazine, Inc.

like him as he is and can respect his right to be dissimilar from you. It means that you allow him to possess his own feelings about matters. It means that you accept his attitudes of the moment, no matter how they may differ from yours.

Although it is highly rewarding to accept another person just as he is, it is not easy to do. You will need to ask yourself some frightening questions. Can I accept him when he looks at life's problems differently than I? Can I accept her when she chooses a different method of coping with problems? Can I permit him to have separate likes and dislikes than I? Can I accept her when she feels angry toward me? Can I respect his right to choose his own beliefs and develop his own values?

Acceptance of others doesn't come easy because of the common resistance to permitting our spouses, our children, our parents, or our friends to feel differently about particular issues or problems than we do. Yet this separateness of the individual, this right each person has to use his experience in his own way and to discover his own meanings, is one of the most priceless possibilities in life.

Does this mean that one should pretend that his mate is perfect? Of course not! Acceptance means that you recognize the imperfections but that you are not going to concern yourself with these areas. Instead, you determine to accept your mate *as he or she is*—faults and all.

Some people feel that they have been practicing acceptance when all they have done is tolerated their mate. They have mustered the strength to restrain criticism but have continued their doleful looks, grimaces, glances, and long painful silences. And each of us can usually sense when we are merely being tolerated rather than being fully accepted. If you can begin to control critical remarks where before you freely stated them, you may well have taken the first step toward full acceptance of others.

An important prerequisite to accepting others at face value is one's ability to accept himself just as he is. Self-acceptance enables us to become more aware of others' needs and to feel less of an urge to rush in and fix up other people. We will become more and more content to be ourselves and to let others be themselves.

Factors Affecting Acceptance

How accepting you are as a person is partly due to temperament. Some people have a great capacity for accepting others. They are calm and easygoing by nature. Aided by their sense of inner security and their high tolerance level, they have real feelings of self-worth. We all like this naturally accepting personality, for we feel comfortable in such a one's presence. We can openly express all our inner feelings without fear of ridicule. We can let our hair down, kick off our shoes, and be our true selves.

Other people are just plain unac-

cepting and often find the behavior of others annoying. They have rigid and strong notions about what conduct is "right" or "wrong." We feel uneasy around such people because we wonder whether we come up to their "standards." Sadly enough, most often religious persons affect us in this manner.

The level of acceptance is affected also by the state of mind. Fewer things bother us when we feel good. However, if we are tired and overworked, are nursing a headache, or are dissatisfied with the day's accomplishments, insignificant things may bother us. Likewise, we are usually much less accepting when friends are visiting in our home or when we are visiting others. For example, conversation and table manners that we would accept at home suddenly bring reprimands.

Acceptance within family groups is much more difficult to achieve than within our circle of friends. If something about a friend irritates us, we can overlook it or find a new friend, but we cannot cross off Grandpa from our list just because he has grown senile. Aunt Martha will still attend all family functions in spite of her selfish demands and need for constant attention. Acceptance between husband and wife can prove even more difficult if one or the other—or both—do not possess a charitable nature. It is hard enough to tolerate senile Grandpa and selfish Aunt Martha, even on occasion, but husband and wife must interact in an accepting manner on a day-to-day basis.

One of the things that I find most difficult to accept in my husband (I didn't have the intestinal fortitude to ask him what he found most difficult to accept about me) is his total unawareness of the passing of time. He can run to a neighbor's to borrow a tool and be gone so long I could file for divorce on grounds of desertion! He can be late for supper even after just phoning me to say he'll be right home. I have come to realize that time means something different to him than it does to me. In my family of "efficiency experts" we were barely allowed bathroom privileges while traveling, and since birth I have been trained to make use of every minute.

Acceptance has taught me to appreciate Harry's easy-going, relaxed nature, which allows him to enjoy frequent present-moment experiences that I bypass because of my drive to produce. Is my "productive" temperament superior to his easy-going one? Should I force Harry into my mold when his entire personality is geared for another speed? Fortunately, acceptance taught me that *different* does not mean *wrong*. I am now free to accept his relaxed manner as an attribute that complements my drive to produce. And fortunately, both of us are not of the same temperament, else we might outdo ourselves competing to produce, or we might be so relaxed that we would accomplish nothing.

We should realize that we cannot feel accepting toward our mates all the time. Some behaviors may always remain unacceptable to some, such as drinking, smoking, gambling, swearing, laziness, dishonesty, or vulgarity. Real people will have real feelings of acceptance and unacceptance toward their spouses during the course of married life.

Furthermore, acceptance does not always mean "liking," but we can view the situation without open hostility. In marriage there are dozens of human differences with which we must learn to live. Whether it is a matter of promptness, church attendance, manner of speech, or personal preference of any kind, through prayer and practice we

A Three-Week Program for Falling Madly in Love (Again)

Criticism, nit-picking, faultfinding, and griping, whether it be aloud or only in the mind, destroy love. God condemns such thinking and instead stresses that we should think with love and thanksgiving about everything: "If there be any virtue, and if there be any praise, *think on these things*" (Philippians 4:8, emphasis supplied).

List ten things you like about your mate and review the list every morning and night, thanking God for each of those blessings.

HIS LIST

"If there by any virtue, and if there be any praise, *think on these things*" (Philippians 4:8).

_____
_____
_____
_____
_____
_____
_____
_____
_____
_____

"In every thing give thanks" (1 Thessalonians 5:18).

HER LIST

"If there be any virtue, and if there be any praise, *think on these things*" (Philippians 4:8).

_____
_____
_____
_____
_____
_____
_____
_____
_____
_____

"In every thing give thanks" (1 Thessalonians 5:18).

can learn to raise our tolerance levels and accept basic differences in individuals.

Common Forms of Unacceptance

Whether you resort to open criticism and belittling remarks or stay with subtle suggestions and tiny hints, it all boils down to unacceptance. Words need not be spoken to convey the message. A disapproving glance, a withering look, or a sigh—all convey an unaccepting attitude.

One of the most common forms of unacceptance is nagging. Wise King Solomon said, "A constant dripping on a rainy day and a cranky woman are much alike! You can no more stop her complaints than you can stop the wind or hold onto anything with oil-slick hands" (Proverbs 27:15, TLB*).

A famous newspaper columnist once wrote: "Many a man loses his grip and gives up the fight to succeed because his wife has wet-blanketed his every hope and aspiration and has taken the heart out of him by her never-ending criticisms and her ceaseless demands to know why he can't make as much money as some other man of her acquaintance or why he can't write a best-seller or get elected to some big office."

A typical nag list from the feminine gender might read as follows: He never fixes anything around the house, never takes me anyplace, won't get up in the morning, watches television too late, gets up too early, won't go to church, spends money foolishly, lives beyond our means, won't talk with me, doesn't understand my feelings, pays no attention to the kids, forgets birthdays and anniversaries, isn't home enough, never says a decent word unless he

wants sex, is stingy with me, is too quiet, leaves the toilet seat up, never picks up his clothes, uses bad grammar, has terrible table manners, drives like a maniac, tells the same jokes over and over, brags too much, swears in front of the children, refuses to exercise, eats too much, spends too much time golfing, doesn't pay bills on time, is too domineering or passive or indecisive.

Nagging is by no means entirely a feminine fault. There are many breeds of men on intelligent levels who are articulate in the art of nagging, although men are more likely to hide their actions under a veil of superior male know-how. Male complaints usually center on sloppy housekeeping, crying spells, dependency on her parents, jealousy, period of silent treatment, spending habits, compulsive lateness, meals never on time, withholding sex as a form of punishment, perfectionist tendencies, negativism toward self, and moodiness.

More often than not, however, a man will criticize rather than nag, but the more a man criticizes, the further away he drives his wife from himself. A wife who is moody, compulsively tardy, or who spends money foolishly rarely responds to criticism. We all grow to resent those who criticize us.

*The Living Bible, Paraphrased (Wheaton: Tyndale House, 1971). Used by permission.

One man who realized that his criticism of his wife's slovenly housekeeping was getting him nowhere decided that he would do her work in addition to his office job. He was not happy over doing double duty, but he practiced this plan for several months until his wife overcame her emotional block that resulted from her own mother, who was a meticulous housekeeper. Whenever she slips back into old habits, he takes over again.

Nagging and Criticism Increase Problems

Even though you may feel that your intentions are good, nagging and criticism create tension in the home. Your mate may become depressed or defensive. She may sulk or pout or even blow up over your suggestions. He may begin to punish you in a dozen insidious ways—to get back at you for not accepting him the way he is. Often communication is cut off. A husband may become openly hostile, bitter, and angry. A wife may become cool, distant, and withdrawn into periods of silence. There may be little sharing. Husband and wife may live under the same roof, yet seldom speak about anything meaningful. In more advanced stages either spouse may seek acceptance outside the home.

Children also suffer from the tension in the home. They may not hear or understand the words, but the atmosphere, the silence, the hurt, the looks, clue the children in that all is not well. With their security so threatened, they begin to worry.

Nagging Kills Love

A number of years ago, Napoleon III, a nephew of Napoleon Bonaparte, fell in love with the Countess of Teba

and married her. Napoleon and his bride had health, wealth, power, fame, beauty, love, and adoration. They were headed for a perfect romance, but their love soon flickered, cooled, and died. Napoleon could make Eugénie an empress, but neither the power of his love nor the might of his throne—nothing in all of France—could keep her from nagging. Jealousy bedeviled her, and suspicion devoured her. She feared that he might be seeing another woman.

What did Eugénie's nagging accomplish? Napoleon, with a soft hat pulled over his eyes and accompanied by one of his intimates, frequently would steal out by a side door at night and betake himself to some fair lady who was expecting him. Eugénie sat on the throne of France. She was one of the most beautiful women in the world. But nothing could keep Napoleon's love alive amid the poisonous bite of nagging.

It is difficult for a man to love a nagging woman, for her nagging reminds him of childhood days when his mother told him "to put on his galoshes, button his coat, and not to talk with his mouth full."

A psychiatrist once asked a nagging wife, "When you tear your husband down all the time, how can you expect him to love you? If he wants to find out what's wrong with him, let him go to a psychiatrist and hate him for telling the truth. You can't afford to provoke his hate."

Women, too, feel crushed under a barrage of criticism and faultfinding. They find little enjoyment in cleaning house, caring for children, or preparing meals for men who criticize their efforts.

Nagging Arouses Defenses

Being accepted as we are is a basic human need, and we search until we find it. Unacceptance wounds the pride, hurts self-esteem, and arouses resentment. One's first line of defense may be a verbal counterattack, or it might come through being stingy, stubborn, lazy, uncooperative, unloving, silent, withdrawn, or through other acts of hostility. The more the other person nags, complains, or criticizes, the more one's resentment may increase. Indeed, an unaccepted person may even begin to spend time away from home in search of someone who does accept him and loves him just as he is. A resentful person often secretly vows to get even somehow.

Nagging Doesn't Work

One woman confessed during a class session on acceptance that she had been trying to change her husband for thirty-five years. She admitted devoting two days out of every week to this project. But she had failed and now felt bitter, tired, and lonely. Complete with tears, she lamented the past thirty-five years spent in a useless pursuit.

Another woman told of listing all her husband's faults on the back side of twelve calendar pages. She admitted

A Few Key Questions

1. Do you spend more time criticizing your mate in your mind than you do at looking at his/her strong points?
2. Does your mate do things that bother you so much that you feel you have to tell him/her about it?
3. Do you talk about your mate in a derogatory manner behind his/her back?
4. Do you have standards for your mate that you can't live up to yourself?
5. Do you pressure your mate to conform to your standards so you can accept him/her more easily?

driving both her husband and her son from the home by her constant attacks. Neither of them changed. The family was reunited only after her husband suffered a heart attack, and the close call shocked her into appreciating his true worth.

Considering the problems created through attempts to change a mate's behavior—the tension, the lack of communication, and the effect on the children—ask yourself: "Is it worth it?" Is changing your mate to suit your ideas more important than a happy home, a loving partner, and emotionally secure children?

The Reason

Why have you attempted to change your partner? If you are honest, you will probably admit that you do it because he or she *needs to change.* Perhaps through feminine insight or masculine logic you have detected areas in your mate's life that need working on so that both of you can be happier. Maybe you even feel it is honorable to help your spouse overcome weak areas and achieve a more acceptable personality. After all, it is *for his or her own good.*

Yet despite these noble-sounding purposes, a basic Christian principle is being violated. The heart of the Christian message revolves around changing ourselves, not *our* ability to change others. Jesus tells us to cast the beam from our own eye before we concentrate on the mote in someone else's eye.

An insidious motive lies behind criticism. We put others down in order to cover up our own feelings of inferiority. By belittling the worth of others we reinforce our own shaky self-esteem.

But putting others down doesn't prove that we have personal worth. Instead we merely place the other person in an inferior position and by so doing

automatically put him on the defensive.

Something should happen to our attitudes when we choose the Christian life-style. We should be able to experience true forgiveness for the mistakes of others. Yet the very fact we are Christians should remind us that God totally accepts us—as sinners. If we don't have to prove our worth to Him, why should we have to prove our worth to others? This knowledge should liberate the Christian. He can develop a greater appreciation for himself and others as he more fully recognizes God's loving acceptance.

Don't Find Fault

Pray don't find fault with the man who limps
    Or stumbles along the road,
Unless you have worn the shoes he wears
    Or struggled beneath his load.
There may be tacks in his shoes that hurt,
    Though hidden away from view,
And the burden he bears, placed on your back,
    May cause you to stumble too.

Don't sneer at the man who is down today,
    Unless you have felt the blow
That caused his fall, or felt the shame
    That only the fallen know.
You may be strong, but still the blows
    That were his, if dealt to you
At the self-same time in the self-same way,
    May cause you to stagger too.

Don't be too harsh with the man who sins
    Or pelt him with words or stones
Unless you are sure, yea, doubly sure,
    That you have no sins of your own.
For who knows, perhaps, if the tempter's voice
    Would whisper softly to you
As it did to him when he went astray
    Would cause you to falter too.

—Vera Barker-Philip

How to Point Out Mistakes—
If You Must

No husband or wife should sit idly by while a mate offends others through actions, words, dress, or body odor. There are times when mistakes should be pointed out, and you may be the only person who cares enough to do this. When this is done properly, your mate should not resent it. Learn just how far you can go with your spouse, where sensitive areas are, and where the difference lies between inciting anger and talking things out. When some wives criticize their husbands even in the slightest way, it signals all-out war. Others can gently point out something they believe will help, and it will be taken kindly.

You may have a legitimate complaint, but your timing may be off. Ask a person to mend his ways only when he or she can do something about it. You may wish to wait until the incident has passed, because often both partners may be too close to a situation to view it with clarity. By allowing the emotions of the moment to cool, you will gain perspective and wisdom.

Guard your manner and tone of voice. Do not speak to your spouse as a parent punishing a small child for naughty behavior. Speak as an equal. Your relationship with one another is more important than any relationship you hold with anyone else on earth, including your children, so guard it carefully.

An English teacher complained to me of her husband's grammar. I personally knew that her husband was a fine Christian church leader, that he held a good job, and that they had many friends. His fault embarrassed only her, and I counseled her to ignore it and to look at his better qualities. The fact is that others are usually more accepting of our mate's idiosyncrasies than we are. After all, they do not have to live with the fault, and this knowledge should free us from part of our drive to reform our mates.

Husband and wife should always feel free to discuss whatever disturbs them, but it shouldn't be in the form of a direct attack. The surest way to weaken affection is to tell someone what is wrong with him too often. Nothing destroys love more quickly than a running account of faults. In order to feel loved we must feel understood, not criticized or condemned.

How to Change Your Mate—
If You Really Want To

Perhaps you are convinced that you should pursue the route of acceptance. You are ashamed of past attitudes and actions, but you wonder whether your mate will make any effort to improve if you practice total acceptance. The thought of facing the future in which he makes no efforts to improve is almost too much for you.

Dr. Murray Bowen, professor of psychiatry at Georgetown University Medical School in Washington, D.C., and a pioneer in the science of family research, says, "The family is a system. Change in one part of the system is always followed by compensatory change in the other parts." According to Dr. Bowen, who has studied families for over twenty years, a problem never belongs to just one person. If a husband is a compulsive worker, perhaps something in his wife invites him to work overtime. If a wife is a lavish spender, maybe something in her husband encourages this extravagance. It isn't easy, of course, to see ourselves as part of a family problem, and it is only human to blame others for our weaknesses. So we fall into the pattern of shifting blame for problems onto our mates.

Furthermore, we often get caught in automatic responses. John comes home late from work without calling. Mary gives him the silent treatment followed by an early-to-bed routine to teach him a lesson and to avoid sex. John gets angry and storms out of the house.

In order for any change to take place in this routine of automatic responses, either John or Mary must pull out of the feeling level and onto the disciplined level of mature thinking. When one is dissatisfied with something the other is doing, rather than whining, criticizing, or nagging, the answer lies in changing routine or habitual behavior.

Let's do an instant replay on John and Mary. John arrives late for supper and hasn't called, but this time Mary plans a new strategy. She feeds the children and puts them to bed on time. When John comes home, Mary reheats the food, and the two of them eat together by candlelight in an atmosphere devoid of silence and anger. She has broken the cycle. John apologizes rather than gets angry.

This will work for you too. It worked for me. One day Harry and I reached an impasse. I suddenly realized that if I was going to keep my husband, *I was going to have to change.* It was either now or never. I completed an internal mental overhaul that began with changing *my* attitudes. I stopped all attempts to change him, to round off rough edges, to suggest what he should do and how he should act. He became a new man. I became a new woman. And we became a new couple. Harry didn't need my advice. He needed my acceptance. And the most amazing thing happened when I gave up the mothering act. As I began to accept him as he was, he put forth real effort to improve certain areas of his personality.

The following threefold axiom may

Work Sheet on Acceptance

1. Express acceptance of your mate in words. Practice what you might say by writing it here.

   _____

   _____

   _____

2. Choose one trait in your spouse that irritates you, and determine to raise your tolerance level toward it. Record that trait here.

   _____ Date: _____

   Check back in a few weeks to see if you are moving toward your goal.

3. Memorize Philippians 2:13-15 and 4:8, 13.

4. Carefully select one change that you want to see God make in your life this week. Write the change here with the date. Date:_____

   Change desired: _____

   Promise claimed: _____

   _____

   Date of answer: _____

5. Copy the statement below and put it in a spot where you will see it a number of times this week.

If I ever want to change my mate, I must stand before the mirror and look at myself a long time.

help shape our new attitudes of acceptance: (1) We can change no one by direct action. (2) We can change only ourselves. And (3) when we change ourselves, others tend to change in response to us.

How to Express Acceptance

Most of us tend to think of acceptance as an attitude that can't be verbalized. Since you love your mate and respond to your mate, you feel that your mate automatically understands that he or she is accepted. Although acceptance originates from within, it must also be demonstrated through actions as well as words. You need to *tell* your mate that you accept him or her *just the way he or she is*.

At first you might find it difficult to express acceptance in words, but this is an important segment of practicing acceptance. You will need to discover individual phrases for expressing it. One of the most welcome expressions might be, "I like you just the way you are." When you say you like a person, it implies that you like him, faults and all. Other good acceptance expressions include: "You are a nice person." "I like the way you do things." "You are everything I had hoped and dreamed you

would be as a person." Mention those specific areas where your mate has fulfilled your hopes and dreams.

Such verbal demonstration of acceptance is a needed part of everyday life when things are running smoothly, but it will be needed more desperately when your mate hurts. At these times he needs to hear meaningful words of acceptance, not just for the things he's done but for him as a person.

At first your words may sound insincere to you, because it will take time for you to reach the full stature of complete acceptance. But you can act from principle and can do it because it fills a human need. You will find that the more you express acceptance, the more it will help you grow toward complete acceptance.

Must You Accept Everything?

Should you become a doormat through the avenue of acceptance? Do you have to accept everything? No. This would mean denying the fact that you are a separate individual, a person to be respected in your own right, a human being with a will of your own.

For example, you need not accept infidelity. Marital partners have the right to expect strict fidelity even in these times of changing moral values. The Word of God, as well as the laws of the land, supports this view. Husbands and wives are within their Christian right in obtaining a divorce when adultery is involved, but a complete self-inventory would save many such marriages. Even a partner with Biblical grounds for divorce can rescue a marriage if he or she is committed to do so. Scripture *permits* but does not *command* divorce on grounds of adultery. Other cases may involve such serious offenses as incest, homosexuality, lesbianism, desertion, nonsupport, mental incapacity, and physical abuse. These need individual attention and professional counseling.

It is difficult to be a Christian under certain circumstances, but God would have us be loving even when we are not loved. We must view unacceptable behavior as God would. He hates the sin in us but loves us, and we can do the same—hate unacceptable behavior in our mates but still love the individual.

A Final Word

Our ultimate desire in marriage should be to create the best possible relationship between two distinctly unique human beings who bring together divergent personality traits. Each should attempt to change what can be altered and improve that which can be corrected. Even then many imperfections will constantly surface. After all possible effort has been expended to work out such difficulties, each person should purpose to accept reality through the most positive outlook possible. Good mental health depends on our ability to accept circumstances that cannot be changed. We can fall apart

over negative situations beyond our ability to control if we allow ourselves to do so. Or we can exercise willpower and resolve to make the best of difficult circumstances.

No one can possibly meet every one of our needs or dreams. Consequently, both partners must settle for a union where reality exists. A successful marriage, then, is not one where perfection reigns, but rather where a couple maintains healthy perspectives when viewing their unresolvable differences.

Further reading you will enjoy...

Andelin, Helen.   *FASCINATING WOMANHOOD*, Chapter 3.
Cooper, Darien.   *YOU CAN BE THE WIFE OF A HAPPY HUSBAND*, Chapter 3.
Dillow, Linda.   *CREATIVE COUNTERPART*, Chapter 5.
Morgan, Marabel.   *TOTAL JOY*, Chapter 3.
Morgan, Marabel.   *TOTAL WOMAN*.
Osborne, Cecil.   *THE ART OF UNDERSTANDING YOUR MATE*.
Renich, Jill.   *TO HAVE AND TO HOLD*, Chapter 2.
Tournier, Paul.   *TO UNDERSTAND EACH OTHER*.

"One of the most prominent reasons why marriages fail is this—husband and wife presume that because they have obtained a license to marry, their success is guaranteed. If through presumption you forget the courtesies by which you won each other, you are likely to wreck your marriage."
—Clovis G. Chappell,
"Sermons From the Parables."

Chapter at a Glance

I. Appreciation

  A. Need for appreciation one of deepest human drives

  B. A man's need for appreciation
    1. Differs from a woman's need
    2. Admire his
      a. Physical qualities
        i. Physique, masculine qualities
        ii. Skills in sports, masculine clothing
      b. Mental qualities
        i. Achievements, skills, and abilities
        ii. Devotion to job, agressiveness
      c. Spiritual qualities
        i. High standards and aspirations
        ii. Noble deeds and sense of honor and duty

  C. A woman's need for appreciation
    1. Admire her
      a. Homemaking

Appreciate Your Mate

At a Compleat Marriage Seminar, I asked the couples to write down at least ten good points about their spouses. I offered a prize to the one who finished the task first. It wasn't long before the winner announced himself, but the number of people who had failed to list even one quality on their paper shocked me. Imagine being married to a person and unable or unwilling to record even one praiseworthy trait! Yet the need for appreciation is one of the deepest human drives.

In the dailiness of married life we tend to take our mates for granted. We grow accustomed to virtues and strengths, and it becomes easy to pounce upon faults and weaknesses that irritate us. We rarely mention admirable qualities but magnify minor irritations.

Admire Him

Admiration and approval meet a man's most basic needs. Women need to be loved. Men need admiration. "If you want a man to keep loving you," Ruth Peale tells wives, "you only have to do one thing—appreciate him and let

Barbara is attractive enough to place in a beauty contest and one of the most creative homemakers I know. But she is now a lonely divorcée. Barbara lost and another woman succeeded because the other woman provided Glen's most basic need—admiration.

A hurt husband wrote Dear Abby to state that he had recently been elected president of his Junior Chamber of Commerce. "I don't recall," he wrote, "ever having worked as hard at anything as I did in the preparation of my acceptance speech. I delivered my speech at the installation banquet, which was attended by the full membership, their wives and guests. After I finished speaking, many of my friends crowded around to shake my hand and congratulate me on how well I had done. Naturally I was pleased. But the one person whose praise I wanted most didn't say one word. She was my wife. This might sound like a small thing, but it was the beginning of my search for 'appreciation.'"

A man appreciates honor and acclaim from others, but there is one individual he wants to impress far more than his business associates, friends, or neighbors—his wife.

To many men physical attributes are very important. Such men want their specifically masculine qualities admired. If your husband feels this way, admire his strength and physique—even in such mundane things as yard work. A young bride told in class how much her husband hated to care for the yard, but after admiring his muscles when he was mowing the lawn, she had no more problem.

Men thrive on admiration. A husband who prefers to remain anonymous parodied a well-known poem this way:

him know you do." This sage bit of homespun advice would save many marriages if women would only practice it.

Over a recent luncheon a friend and I took up this very point in connection with her marriage. "Nancy," Barbara began, "this was the most important lesson I learned from your classes. I didn't understand Glen's needs for admiration. As I look back on our marriage, I can see where I must have hurt his pride deeply by ignoring his abilities and not providing the admiration he needed."

If with pleasure you are viewing
Any work a man is doing,
If you like him or you love him,
   Tell him now.
Don't withhold your approbation,
Till the preacher makes oration,
And he lies with snowy lilies on his brow.
For no matter how you shout it,
He won't really care about it,
He won't know how many teardrops
   You have shed.
If you think some praise is due him,
Now's the time to slip it to him,
For he cannot read his tombstone
   When he's dead.

Courage and devotion to his lifework also deserve admiration. And what about the check he brings home regularly? Many women accept financial support for a lifetime without due appreciation.

Note what he likes to do with his special talents, aptitudes, and skills. Friends of ours own a cabin at nearby Bass Lake, and we often join the crowd that gathers there on holiday weekends. We can count on Dick as host to prepare his specialty once during the weekend—omelets stuffed with mushrooms, green olives, and cheese—served with his own recipe of cheese bread. Talents like these deserve recognition. Whether a man is mechanically minded, proficient in mathematics, or an avid reader, a wife should see to it that she satisfies his need for appreciation.

Does he leave you free to develop your own interests? share the car with you? occasionally help with the dishes and take out the garbage? withhold complaints when you're late with dinner? remember anniversaries and birthdays without being prompted? Such courtesies require appreciation.

The Kindness Check

If you have been aware that you are caustic, sarcastic, or cutting in your speech to your mate, try The Kindness Check. That is, every time you say something to your mate ask yourself, "Is that kind?" If not, apologize and ask God to help you say something kind instead.

Obviously this is not an easy assignment. You may find it hard, particularly the first week. But if you will consistently practice The Kindness Check, caustic communication in your home will fade, and a genuine renewal of your affection for one another will increase.

Record your progress on The Kindness Check after one, two, three, and four weeks.

1. _____   3. _____

2. _____   4. _____

In Ephesians 4:32 Paul says, "Be kind to each other, tenderhearted, forgiving one another, just as God has forgiven you because you belong to Christ" (TLB *). Have these attitudes been demonstrated in your home? What does it mean to be kind to one another? How can we show kindness toward each other in marriage?

During the next five minutes jot down how you can put this passage into practice in your own home during the next week.

_____

_____

_____

_____

---

*Taylor. The Living Bible, Paraphrased (Wheaton: Tyndale House, 1971). Used by permission.

Does he devote time and energy toward being a superior husband and proper father? If he offers to take little Billy with him on an errand to relieve you for a time, appreciation will reinforce his desire to spend time with his son.

This chapter encourages men to woo their wives with small gifts and remembrances from time to time, but a woman may crush her husband's efforts at gift-giving by showing her ingratitude through disappointment or criticism. It took me a while to learn how to accept gifts from Harry. I am practical and thrifty by nature, and I worry about finances when he gives me extravagant presents. One anniversary he presented me with an expensive steam iron. Because our anniversary falls immediately after Christmas, I questioned his wisdom in purchasing this for me when he had just spent so much at Christmas. My mother, who was visiting for the holidays, overheard my reaction and took me aside to teach me a lesson I had not yet learned.

Returning a gift, exchanging it for something else, or putting it away without using it are discourtesies nearly unforgivable. A garment that doesn't fit, however, may be exchanged for another size. If you don't like something, use it for a time and then put it away. The principle involved is to appreciate the giver, not the gift. Choose your words carefully in order to show appreciation for the thoughtfulness behind the gift.

Appreciate Her

Women also have a natural need for appreciation, which too few men realize. A man takes professional pride in his occupation and is rewarded periodically with raises, promotions, and bonuses. A woman's work centers around household chores, well-

scrubbed children, and her husband. But unlike a man, she cannot look forward to promotions, raises, paychecks, or bonuses at home. Yet many times a few kind words of appreciation from her husband would soothe the irritations of her day.

When a woman does not feel appreciated, she may deliberately try to provoke attention. Many tearful tantrums and staged scenes may well be desperate attempts for attention. Other women go one step further in their desperate attempts to cope with situations that provide no rewards. They develop headaches, dizziness, backaches, and complaints about endless fatigue. Husbands of such wives could save themselves a small fortune on medical bills by whispering a few well-timed words of love and appreciation along with a few dollars' worth of flowers.

During our courtship I could not have asked for more from Harry in the romance department—flowers, corsages, long-distance phone calls, letters every day, pictures, cards, dinners. *And he continues these attentions yet.* He has never forgotten a birthday or anniversary, let alone Mother's Day and Valentine's Day. But he goes far beyond these traditional occasions. He loves to surprise me. One evening when I had a group of friends over for a crafts class, a large box wrapped in beautiful paper with matching bow appeared on the kitchen table. No occasion, no reason outside of the fact that he enjoys surprising me.

When I return from speaking engagements, he greets me at the airport with a "happy-to-have-you-home" card on the front seat of the car along with some candy or nuts. Sometimes it will be only my favorite candy bar, but there will be something. At home I can count on another card on my pillow and

maybe another surprise or two around the house.

And my chivalrous, attentive, romantic husband is doing much more than just keeping me happy. He is modeling for his observant teenage sons. Harry's consistent example will give the world two more men who understand a woman's needs and who in *every* way will make fine husbands and fathers.

Then, too, a woman needs to hear over and over again from her husband just how attractive she is. Compliments on her hair, figure, or her dress are always in order. Especially is this true as she passes forty. We cannot ignore the fact that a younger woman can appear very attractive to older men. Consequently, a woman painfully recognizes what the passing years are doing to her face, hair, and figure. She needs reassurance that she is still attractive, interesting, and sexy.

Many women complain that their husbands show attention or affection only when they want to engage in sexual relations. A wife who never receives attention except during intercourse will grow to reject her husband and their sexual relationship; so the man who wants his wife to welcome his sexual

Pass the Praise

(A plan of action for him)

To a woman the magic of a present is in the joy of the surprise and anticipation more than in the contents of the package. Make your gifts inexpensive but personal. It's the spark of insight on your part that will do the trick. By what you choose she knows you have noticed what she likes or needs. And more than anything else that's what communicates your love.

No. 1: SAY IT WITH FLOWERS. Stop by the florist's and pick up a single long-stemmed rose for her. Present it at the door or at dinner with the comment, "I thought of you today and just wanted to say, 'I love you.'"

No. 2: CALL HER THREE TIMES THIS WEEK—for no other reason than to say, "I love you and am glad I'm married to you."

No. 3: MAKE YOUR OWN ANNIVERSARY OR BIRTHDAY CARD, rather than buying one. No matter how crude it is, it will be guaranteed a cherished place in her memory and scrapbook.

Remember, the magic of gift giving is that you thought of and cared about her when you weren't *expected to.* Put some "days to remember" on your calendar over the next six months, and give often. You'll love what happens to her and *you!*

Now list some specific and creative ways you can express appreciation to your wife:

1. _____

2. _____

3. _____

4. _____

5. _____

advances will often take her hand in the car, while walking, or even in church, and give her a special smile. When out socially, he can make it a point to single her out several times during the evening. How I love it when Harry gives me a special wink across a crowded room.

These legitimate female needs are met by superior marital partners, for they know that a little imagination and planning can melt a woman's heart. It costs so little, but it can soothe a multitude of misunderstandings.

How to Be a More Appreciative Person

Study your mate. Mrs. Ruth Peale says: "If I could give one piece of advice to young brides, and only one, it would be this: 'Study your man. . . . Study his likes and dislikes, his strengths and weaknesses, his moods and mannerisms. Just loving a man is fine, but it's not enough. To live with one successfully you have to know him, and to know him you have to study him.' "

Good advice for both partners.

When you undertake such a study, you will learn what upsets your spouse as well as how to make laughter. You'll understand when your mate needs encouragement as well as when he or she needs to calm down and reflect more rationally.

This study of your mate should never stop, for if it does, your spouse may outgrow you as the years go by. However, if you really study your mate over the years, you may come to know him or her almost better than you know yourself.

The divorce courts are full of spouses who didn't take the time, expend the energy, or care enough to study their mates. They failed to meet needs and observe certain warning signals while they still had the time to do something constructive for their relationship.

Look at your mate. Develop your powers of observation so that you can detect in your mate new attitudes and abilities and dormant or unrecognized qualities that you can compliment. Forget self and look at things from another point of view. As you become more accepting you will be able to understand why your mate acts and thinks differently from you. As you become more understanding, your mate will reveal more to you, and new behavior patterns will crop up for you to study.

Show a willingness to participate, at least occasionally, in activities your mate enjoys. Wives would love to have their husbands show an interest in their decorating projects, school and church activities, or a short shopping spree. Husbands may be sports enthusiasts, gardeners, or sport car fans, but the wives may never show any interest in these areas. Sometimes even a pretended interest can become a real one.

Listen to your mate. What a wonderful way to discover each other! We

Pass the Praise

(A plan of action for her)

You have spent some time thus far attempting to change negative attitudes into more positive ones, as well as dwelling on your husband's admirable qualities. Now let's plan some ways of passing the praise. Here are a few ideas to get you started.

No. 1: HOLD AN ELECTION. Tell your man he has just been voted "Husband and Father of the Year" by you and the children.

No. 2: BUY A CONTEMPORARY CARD that expresses how you feel about him, and send or give it to him.

No. 3: COMPLIMENT HIM—on his brains, his looks, his abilities, his fathering, his conversation, or anything he does well.

Now you're on your own. List specific and creative ways you can express appreciation to your man:

1. _____

2. _____

3. _____

4. _____

5. _____

crave a sounding board against which we can test ideas, hopes, dreams, ambitions, problems, and inner conflicts that are difficult to solve alone. We all need someone to whom we can confide our innermost thoughts and feelings without fear of ridicule and rejection. Show an interest and ask questions your partner will enjoy answering. Everyone loves a good listener.

How to Express Appreciation

Express it verbally. Some people think of love and appreciation as feelings and attitudes, and they don't know how to express them verbally. Other people hold back words because they assume that their partners know their feelings, as if they were mind readers.

A recent project gathered hundreds of husbands and wives together in small group sessions. There they talked openly—some for the first time in their married lives—about the qualities they loved and valued in each other. "It was amazing," one young wife said. "Pete and I had always more or less assumed we were in love. But when we actually said why and how it made us feel inside, we discovered our love was far deeper than we had imagined."

At first you may feel a little foolish expressing appreciation in words, but keep at it. Your mate needs to *hear* you say how you feel in your heart. You may feel that you have been expressing appreciation in other ways—by keeping house, bringing home a paycheck, or by preparing favorite foods. But these actions do not fill the need for expressing your appreciation in words.

Identify a specific quality. When you express admiration, avoid generalizations that arouse curiosity or perplexity about what a person is trying to say. One woman told her husband that he was a "manly sort of man." He began

to quiz her on what she meant, and she couldn't think of one quality. Express appreciation for a particular deed or characteristic when it is evident—a hairdo, a courtesy, a new coat, her figure. This way what you say will be taken at face value without further questioning.

Avoid flattery. Flattery and appreciation differ. One is sincere, and the other is insincere. One is selfish, and the other is unselfish. One is universally admired, and the other is universally condemned. Someone has said, "Don't be afraid of the enemies who attack you. Be afraid of those who flatter you." Appreciation and praise are based on character traits and actions.

Praise daily. Develop the reputation for being an appreciative partner. Make sure that a day never goes by without an opportunity to admire some good quality in each family member. Expressing affection and appreciation day in and day out is one of the most effective techniques for smoothing the rough edges of family life.

The Effects of Appreciation

Appreciation is a powerful motivator in changing behavior. How does it work? In an old fable the wind and sun began quarreling about who was stronger. The wind said: "I'll prove I am. See that old man down there with a coat? I bet I can get his coat off quicker than you can." So the sun went behind a cloud, and the wind blew until it was almost a tornado, but the harder it blew the tighter the old man wrapped his coat about him. Finally the wind calmed down and gave up. When the sun came out from behind the clouds and smiled kindly on the old man, he presently mopped his brow and pulled off his coat. The sun then told the wind that gentleness and friendliness were always stronger than fury and force.

It changes behavior. Instead of criticizing when your husband or wife does something you don't like, comment favorably when they say or do something of which you approve. Called positive reinforcement, this technique also works wonders on children and is fully described in the companion book, *The Compleat Parent.*

Poet Robert Browning knew how to put positive reinforcement into practice. His love and appreciation for Elizabeth Barrett became the breath of her life. One of eleven children, she suffered under a tyrannical, oppressive father. His rages and severe control over a period of time confined the sensitive Elizabeth to her bed with an accumulation of ills. So went her life until when she was nearly forty she met Robert Browning.

He did not see her as a sickly, middle-aged invalid, but rather as a beautiful, talented spirit waiting to walk out of a darkened room into the sunshine. He helped her develop unseen capacities, to blossom forth, and be known to the world. He lifted her from a morbid existence by appreciating her fine qualities and by recognizing the unused potential lying dormant within her. Her rare artistry for expression produced such works as her *Sonnets From the Portuguese,* which included the exquisite "How Do I Love Thee?" a word portrait of the transformation Robert Browning had performed in her life.

One woman complained that her husband was so chronically thoughtless and so immersed in his business affairs that he seldom even remembered her birthday. "I could have tried to force him into changing his ways," she said, "but it seemed to me this would only make matters worse. Instead, I waited for the first chance I had to praise him for some small act of thoughtfulness. When he finally brought home a book I had asked for four times, I thanked him as if it were a fur coat! He looked at me oddly, but I could see he was pleased. I did this a few more times, and gradually he began to want to think about me because he enjoyed being appreciated."

Your mate will respond much the same. Instead of nagging him to take out the garbage, ask him to lend you his strong arms. Instead of growling at her when a button drops off a shirt, tell her what a marvelous homemaker she is. Such tactics prompt others into striving to do their best.

It reinforces a positive self-image. Husbands need someone with whom they can share their ideas of how things ought to be. They need to test and sample responses from their wives. They need someone to confirm their ideas in concurrence with their view of themselves. This confirmation, when it comes from someone who cares, reinforces their self-image and makes them feel more confident and secure.

Young husbands just beginning their careers particularly need this approval. Filled with ideas, proposals, confidence, and zest, they quickly detect outmoded methods of doing things. They itch to prove that there is a better way, but often their colleagues may be too busy with their own plans, or they may throw a wet blanket on new ideas. These young husbands need someone to reinforce their mental picture of themselves when they get their turn at the helm.

Women also need appreciation to establish a sense of self-worth. The traditional responsibilities of women are now being ridiculed. Some critics actually view women who raise children and maintain a home as second-class citizens. As a result, women who are dedicated to their responsibilities often begin feeling as though something is wrong with them—that they are dumb or stupid or unnecessary to society. Homemakers need to know that they are respected and appreciated for the contribution they make toward a smooth-running family. Nothing on earth can build the self-respect of a wife more quickly than for her husband to reaffirm her value as a person, a wife, a mother, and a homemaker.

In marriage we are always reacting to one another—positively, negatively, or passively. We have the ability to heal one another or hurt one another—to restore or deplete, to help or hinder. We can make our mates feel important, alive, and worthy, or we can make them feel inadequate and useless. The best method to use in healing, restoring, and helping is appreciation.

Further reading you will enjoy...

Andelin, Helen. *FASCINATING WOMANHOOD,* Chapter 4.
Dillow, Linda. *CREATIVE COUNTERPART,* Chapter 6.
Morgan, Marabel. *TOTAL JOY,* chapters 4 and 6.
Morgan, Marabel. *TOTAL WOMAN,* chapters 5 and 7.
Peale, Ruth. *THE ADVENTURES OF BEING A WIFE,* chapters 3 and 11.
Spry, Toni. *THE FULFILLED WOMAN,* Chapter 6.

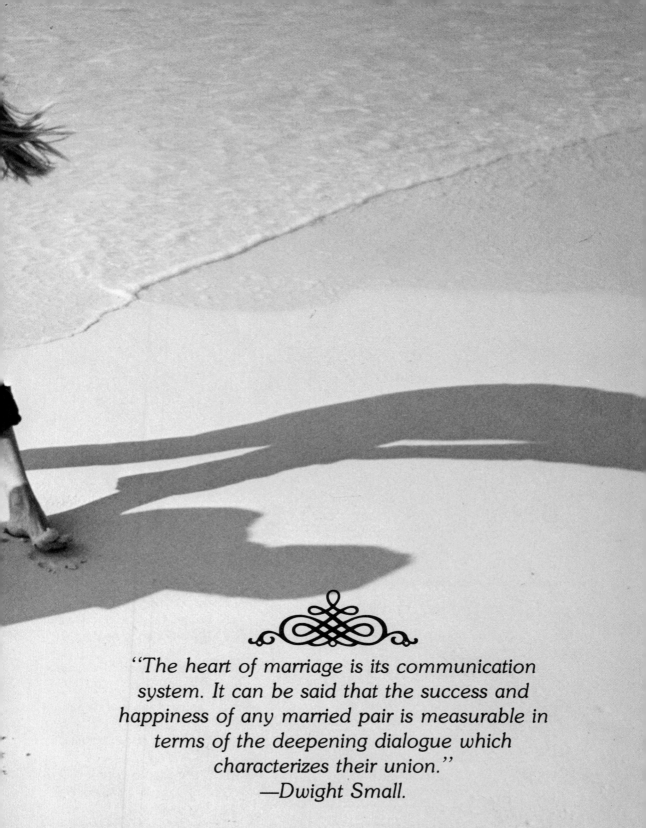

"The heart of marriage is its communication
system. It can be said that the success and
happiness of any married pair is measurable in
terms of the deepening dialogue which
characterizes their union."
—Dwight Small.

Chapter at a Glance

Communicate With Your Mate

"I don't understand what has happened to us," explains George. "Before we were married we had so much to talk about. Now we never talk. Janet says I never tell her anything, and she wouldn't listen if I did. She isn't interested in anything I'm interested in."

Experts claim that one of the most serious problems in marriage and a prime cause of divorce lies in the inability or reluctance of couples to communicate. Many of these couples know they aren't communicating, but they aren't sure exactly what it is they are or are not supposed to do. Although communication is a complex process, it isn't complicated.

Communication in marriage is complete when a couple can handle three principles consistently: (1) when they can effectively utilize the fundamentals involved in speaking and listening, (2) when they can resolve conflicts through constructive methods, and (3) when they spend time on a daily basis in an intimate sharing of feelings.

What Communication Is

We often assume that if someone's lips are moving, communication is taking place. But the two-way street of

---

B. Effective methods of listening
C. Rules for effective listening
    1. Maintain good eye contact
    2. Sit attentively
    3. Act interested
    4. Show agreement and understanding
    5. Ask well-phrased questions
    6. Listen more—talk less

IV. Solving Conflicts
A. Rules for solving conflicts constructively:
    1. Choose the best time and place

    2. Say it straight
    3. Stay on the subject
    4. Show respect
    5. List the solutions
    6. Evaluate the solutions
    7. Choose the most acceptable solution
    8. Implement the decision

V. Intimate Communication

The Five Levels of Communication

John Powell, in his book *Why I Am Afraid to Tell You Who I Am*, describes five levels on which we can communicate, and an understanding of these levels is essential.

Level 5: Small Talk. At this level shallow conversation takes place, such as, "How are you?" "What have you been doing?" "How are things going?" Such conversation borders on the meaningless, but it can sometimes be better than embarrassed silence. When communication remains on this level, it is boring and leads to frustration and resentment in marriage.

Level 4: Factual Conversation. At this level, information is shared, but there are no personal comments along with it. You tell what has happened but do not reveal how you feel about it. A wife may observe her husband leaving the house after dinner and ask, "Where are you going?" and he can give a factual answer, "Out." Men are more apt to settle for this level than women, as they are often less able to express their feelings.

Level 3: Ideas and Opinions. Real intimacy begins here, for on this level you risk exposing your own thoughts, feelings, and opinions. Because you feel free to express yourself and verbalize personal ideas, your partner has a better chance to know you intimately.

Level 2: Feelings and Emotions. Communication at this level describes what is going on inside you—how you feel about your partner or a situation. You verbalize feelings of frustration, anger, resentment, or happiness. If you honestly share with your partner in a give-and-take manner, showing interest in his feelings as well as in expressing your own, this level will enrich and enlarge your relationship. You will feel worthy, noticed, loved, appreciated, and safe in your partner's affections. You will gain flashes of insight into your partner's character that will give you real understanding of how he thinks and feels. A good combination is to alternate between the levels of ideas/opinions and feelings/emotions.

Level 1: Deep Insight. Rare insightful moments will occur when you are perfectly in tune with another in understanding, depth, and emotional satisfaction. Usually a peak experience or something deeply personal is related. Communication about such experiences often makes a deep impression on both parties and enriches the relationship. Mutual sharing of personal ideas and feelings is the ultimate goal in marital communication.

What level of communication occurs in your marriage now? Do you want and need a deeper and more intimate sharing?

conversation comprises the giving and receiving of information. Moreover, it involves more than talking. It is the receiving or listening process as well. To this twofold process we should add a third dimension—understanding. Frequently we think we understand what our mates are saying, but what we hear is not what is meant. We want the other person not only to listen to what we have to say but also to understand.

The Conversing Angle of Communication

We spend approximately 70 percent of our waking hours in communication—speaking or listening, reading or writing. Thirty-three percent of this time is devoted to talking. This element of our time becomes very important, for talk brings people together in a relationship.

The avenue of speech goes beyond just the exchange of words or information. Through talking we can express our feelings, convey our emotions, clarify our thinking, reinforce our ideas, and make contact with others. It is a pleasant way of passing time, getting to know one another, releasing tension,

and expressing opinions. The most basic function of speaking, then, is not the giving of information but the establishing of a relationship with others. The quality of this relationship will depend a great deal on the ability of each person to express himself verbally.

Barrier to Effective Speaking

Many barriers block effective speech.

The "solution sender" weights down his speech with orders, directions, and commands. "Get over here." "Hang up your clothes." "Hurry up." Warnings and threats comprise more solutions. "If you *ever* do that again, I'll . . ." Another is moralizing. "Don't you know enough not to . . ." Most of us resent being told we *must, should,* or *better* do something.

Many of us resort to "put-downs" in spite of the fact that we know what it feels like to be put down. Put-downs judge, criticize, and blame: "That's not a bad idea, considering you thought of it." They name call, ridicule, and shame: "You're a slob." They interpret, diagnose, and psychoanalyze: "You only say that because . . ." They attempt to teach and instruct: "Honey, we

Exercise in Nonverbal Communication

Let's consider what some nonverbal or voice behaviors might mean. Look at the following list and try to give a meaning for each behavior. Share your list of meanings with your mate.

What does it mean when a person . . .

It says . . .

1. nods his/her head up and down?

2. smiles slightly?

3. speaks in a loud, harsh voice?

4. suddenly opens his/her eyes wide?

5. keeps eyes lowered when speaking to you?

6. yawns during a conversation?

7. shrugs his/her shoulders?

8. sits rigid and upright in a chair?

9. folds arms tightly across the chest?

10. wrings his/her hands?

11. starts to turn pale?

12. speaks in a low, monotonous voice?

13. fiddles with shirt collar or scarf?

14. slouches in a chair?

15. hits his/her forehead with hands?

16. speaks in a very halting or hesitant voice?

shouldn't leave our towels on the floor."

Dr. James Dobson tells of a game husbands and wives play. He calls it Assassinate the Spouse. In this destructive game the player (usually a husband, he notes) attempts to punish his wife by ridiculing and embarrassing her in front of their friends. He can hurt her when they are alone, but in front of friends he can really cut her down. If he wants to be exceptionally cruel, he'll let the guests know how stupid and ugly she is—the two aspects where she is the most vulnerable. Bonus points are awarded if he can reduce her to tears.

Then there is the "corrector." For example, while the husband tells a story to friends, his wife helps him keep the facts straight.

"We left on Sunday night . . ."

"Oh, honey, I think it was Thursday night just before the holiday."

"OK, we left Thursday right after the kids got home from school."

"No, dear, it was late that evening when we got away. Remember, the kids came home and we had a big supper before we left."

"Well, anyway, we left and drove straight to Los Angeles, and . . ."

"Honey, are you sure we went there first? I thought we . . ."

A corrector has a compulsion to concentrate on proper reporting. Such remarks are often attempts to draw attention to self, and they show a lack of sensitivity in allowing someone else to tell a story the way he perceives and remembers it.

The "judge" tries to second-guess what will come next. A wife might say, "They are having a really good movie at the church Wednesday night."

Her husband doesn't wait to see what point she is going to make, but he cuts her off with, "Yes, we're not going."

The "monologuer" has a compulsive need to talk and frequently insists on having the last word. He can't bear to be corrected, and so he maintains a know-it-all attitude. Often monologuers have a desperate need to be popular, but the more they monopolize conversations, the more they bore others and cut themselves off from forming close attachments.

The "silent treatment" uses silence as a weapon or a form of control. Both husbands and wives use it, but usually in different ways. When a man is silent, strong emotions such as fear or anger are building up inside. A woman usually uses silence to get even for some injustice done to her or when she reaches the stage of total despair and desperation. The silent treatment may be given because one refused to listen last time, or the silent one may be suffering from a deep hurt. Some Christians feel that it isn't right to say what they think. Others resort to silence for the children's sake. But this bottling of emotion takes its toll physically, mentally, and spiritually.

The "silent husband," according to some marriage counselors, lies behind one half of all the troubled marriages they encounter. Many women complain that their husbands don't talk to them and cannot be prodded into it. The husband communicates primarily on the "small talk" or "factual" level.

Several attitudes account for male silence. Some men, particularly workaholics, consider little in life but productivity to be of value. Their answer to all of life's problems is action, not talk. Other men are so dogmatic and authoritarian that they refuse to speak further on a subject once they have handed down an edict. Still others detest discussing what they term "trivia."

When a woman experiences a problem or feels strong emotion she wants to talk and let her feelings out. A man under the stress of emotion usually clams up, closes the gate, and retreats within himself because he has been trained since birth to keep tight control on his emotions. He will cut himself off from anything that differs from the logical and detached way of life to which he has become accustomed. And as he grows older he grows tougher so that his peers won't detect any sign of softness or emotion.

Whenever feelings well up within him, a man's automatic response is to turn them off, *especially in the presence of a woman.* If he gets angry and lashes out at her, he isn't a gentleman. If he cries, it is a sign of weakness. Consequently he uses silence as a method of escaping from his feelings, failing to understand how this maddens his wife, when her aim is to get it all out in the open.

However, few men really want to remain silent. Most every man likes to talk as much as his wife, although usually about different types of things. But chiding or needling will drive even the best-intentioned man to withdraw even further. He wants and needs a companion with whom he feels secure and safe from ridicule. A man will respond to a woman he trusts.

Effective Methods of Speaking

An old adage says, "Treat your family like friends and your friends like family." Most of us need to make concentrated effort to speak as politely to our spouses as we do to our friends. Often familiarity leads to neglect and disregard, and soon we pull out all the stops and feel that we can say and do anything we like. "After all," we rationalize, "it's only family."

How are you coming across to your mate? Does your speech sting with sarcasm? Can you state what you mean? Do you show an interest in your mate as a person, let him know that you care? Have you tried using I-messages in your conversation? They identify your actual feelings and report them openly, honestly, and kindly to your mate. I-messages are particularly useful when you feel irritated with something your mate does. Rather than responding

"You <u>couldn't</u> have been listening. If you'd been listening, you'd be mad."

Drawing by Hoff, © 1950, 1978, The New Yorker Magazine, Inc.

with hostile words and actions, say, "I feel irritated because . . ."

Compare the different reactions to these two messages sent by wives after their husbands refused to take them out to dinner.

Wife No. 1: "You're so inconsiderate! All I do is slave for you, and you never think of anyone but yourself. All you want to do is watch TV. You make me sick!"

Wife No. 2: "I really need a break tonight. I've been cooped up in the house all week. I need to be alone with

you to communicate on an adult level."

Wife No. 2 tells only how she feels, a fact her husband can hardly argue with. Wife No. 1 blames, judges, and puts down her husband. This gives him ammunition for an argument and will probably cause him to become more stubborn and defensive than before.

I-messages quickly eliminate the attack and defense in mutual name-calling and reciprocal blaming. If a wife reminds her husband in an accusing way that he has plenty of time to work on the camper but no time to keep the yard in shape, he will probably react something like this: "There you go again. Always hounding me about that yard. Nag, nag, nag."

A direct report of her feelings through an I-message would ease the situation: "I'm becoming more and more irritated over this unkept yard that I must look at all day. I'd like to sit down and talk about it while I am still able to control my irritation." She reported her personal feelings without put-downs and without telling him what to do. He is now free to accept or reject her opinion.

More examples of how to use the I-message follow:

The wife is watching television in bed when her husband wants to sleep. "I've had a hectic day, and I'm too tired to watch television with you. I'm going to turn over and go to sleep now."

The husband buries himself behind the newspaper as soon as he gets home from work, but his wife says, "I need a little intimate conversation tonight because I feel all bottled up inside. I really could use a little time to talk with you."

I-messages bring some startling results. Spouses are surprised to learn how the other really feels about matters. Often their replies might sound like this: "I didn't know it even bothered you," or "Why didn't you say something before?" We often underestimate the

Effective Speaking Rules

1. *Choose the right time to communicate with your spouse.* Your subject may be well-taken, but your timing may be off. If you have something personal from levels one or two to share, don't unload just as a man walks in the door after spending a hectic day at the office and forty-five minutes on the freeway. If you want to talk with your wife about cutting down on food expenses, don't begin just as she is serving a meal over which she has slaved. Select a time when your mate can respond pleasantly.

2. *Develop a pleasant tone of voice.* It isn't always what you say, but how you say it that counts. It is soothing to be around someone with a soft, calm voice. If you want your mate to enjoy the sound of your voice, make sure you are easy to listen to.

3. *Be clear and specific.* Many misunderstandings arise from muddled talk. Try to think as you speak, and state clearly what you mean. Couples can solve the problem of muddled communication by making "a statement of intent." For example, "I would like to invite the Browns over for dinner Sunday. Do you mind?"

4. *Be positive.* In many homes 80 percent of all communication is negative. These families become so used to hearing faultfinding, blaming, judging, name-calling, and other negative elements that such behavior becomes normal. Be less negative and more positive and appreciative.

5. *Be courteous and respectful of your mate's opinion.* You can do this even when you don't agree. Care as much about his comfort as you do about your own. And be willing to listen. No more than 50 percent of your communication should be spent with *your* talking.

6. *Be sensitive to the needs and feelings of your mate.* Develop patience and sensitivity in responding to what your mate says. If he hurts, you can understand his hurt and even hurt with him. Tune into the needs and feelings of fear, anger, despair, and anxiety of your loved one. Likewise, if he is happy over a new development, enjoy his happiness with him.

7. *Develop the art of conversation.* A recent study conducted at Cornell University showed that the more time husbands and wives spend talking with each other, the more likely they are to report a high level of marital satisfaction. Happier husbands and wives just naturally have more to say to one another than miserable ones. Conversation is an art, and opportunities to develop it should be encouraged. Discussion on interesting subjects enriches a relationship.

willingness of our mates to be more considerate. If you really want to have your feelings recognized, you must *continually* communicate them directly until you are understood.

The Listening Angle of Communication

"Faulty listening," says one psychoanalyst, "is usually at the root of most marital communication problems. Sometimes it merely causes annoyance or irritation. But when a person is talking about something important, trying to get a problem resolved, or seeking emotional support, poor listening can have disastrous results."

Yet most of us prefer to talk rather than listen. We enjoy expressing our ideas and telling what we know and how we feel about matters. We expend more energy in expressing our own thoughts than in giving full attention when others are expressing theirs. Listening seems like such a simple thing to do, yet most of us are poor listeners because listening is hard work.

What are some of the problems in listening?

One couple sought counseling because their conversations turned into arguments. Each evening the husband would try to unload the events of his pressure-packed job. His wife would tell of coping with three active youngsters. Each was looking for sympathy, support, and solutions to problems. Yet neither had the patience to listen with understanding but, instead, eagerly jumped in with his or her own complaints.

Barriers to Effective Listening

The "bored listener" has heard it all before. When Mr. J rehashes complaints about his job, Mrs. J says to herself, "Here we go again," and puts her brain in neutral. Yet on occasion when Mr. J says something new and looks for support and encouragement from his wife he isn't likely to get it.

A "selective listener" picks out bits and pieces of conversation that interest him and rejects the rest. For instance, a husband may be watching the six o'clock news while his wife is talking. Most of what she says goes in one ear and out the other, but when she mentions spending money he becomes all ears. Other people do not want to hear anything disagreeable, upsetting, or different—Ernie's behavior at school or more expenses on the car. We do not gain anything by rejecting what we do not wish to hear. In many situations we need all the facts in order to make a decision.

A "defensive listener" twists everything said into a personal attack on self. One wife casually remarked to her husband that the new dress lengths left her with nothing to wear. Although she never mentioned purchasing a new wardrobe, he flew into a rage because he felt that her remarks were directed toward a lack of his ability to earn a living. A hurt wife gave her husband the "silent treatment" all evening because

Exercise in Listening for Feelings

We communicate to others much more than our words imply. Behind our words often lie our *feelings.* Below are some typical feelings shared by mates. Read each statement carefully, listening for feelings. In the space write the feeling you heard. Some situations may contain more than one feeling. If so, write down the main feelings you heard.

Example: Go away and leave me alone. I don't ever want to talk to you again. You don't care about me anyway. Anger, hurt, resentment

1. I'm so glad I'm married to you. _____

2. I think I understand, but what if I do it wrong? I have a knack for doing the wrong thing at the right time. _____

3. Why can't I buy it? I have as much right to buy something new as you do! _____

4. I get so behind in my work. I can never get it all done. What will I do? _____

5. This was the longest day in history. I didn't have anything to do. _____

6. Hank wants to move to a new home across town, but I don't want to move. _____

7. Thank you. That was a very thoughtful thing for you to do. _____

8. Sometimes I feel that no one cares about me. _____

9. I don't know what to do. Should I go back to college or get a part-time job? _____

10. I shouldn't have said that. It was the wrong thing to say. _____

11. Do you like my new outfit, honey? I made it myself. _____

12. Trying to get to the doctor these days is as difficult as getting an appointment with the President. _____

she felt that his disgust with the children's table manners was a personal attack on her ability to train them properly.

"Interrupters" spend their time not listening to what is being said but in forming a reply. Interested only in their own ideas, they pay little attention to the words of others and wait only for a split second when they can break in with, "Oh, that's nothing. You should hear what happened to me." Or, "That reminds me of . . ."

Another hazard is the "insensitive listener"—one who cannot catch the feeling or emotion behind words. One young wife asks her husband to take her out to dinner. She does not need to be taken out to dinner as much as she needs reassurance that he still loves her and is willing to make the effort to please her. If he tells her bluntly that they can't afford it or he is too tired, he hasn't listened to the meaning behind her request.

Effective Methods of Listening

Emphasis on effective listening is not new, but until recently more emphasis had been placed on the ability and willingness to speak freely than on effective listening. Today, however, some schools teach listening skills along with the three Rs. Corporations are encouraging employees to avail themselves of certain courses to improve their listening skills. Family counselors are emphasizing the importance of how to listen within the family circle. Following are some techniques suggested by a collection of experts to help you and your mate enhance your listening abilities.

Be alert to body language. We communicate by the spoken word, but we also communicate by what we do not say. Fifty-five percent of what we communicate is expressed through facial expressions—a pout, a sigh, a grimace, or a squint of the eyes. Such body language speaks louder than words. Other nonverbal messages are caught through body postures or gestures—a nervous tapping of the foot, tightly clenched teeth, or a motion of irritation. Such behavior patterns offer keys to feelings behind the words and set up barriers before conversation begins.

The door opener. A good listening technique is found in responding with a "door opener" or the invitation to say more. These responses do not communicate any of your own ideas or feelings, yet they invite your mate to share his thoughts. Some of the simplest "door openers" are: "I see." "You don't say." "Tell me more." "I'd be interested in your point of view." "Tell me the whole story." In this way you encourage the other person to talk and do not give the idea that you can hardly wait to snatch the conversation away. They convey respect by implying: "I might learn something from you. Your ideas are important to me. I am interested in what you have to say."

Active listening. "Deliberate listening" is the ability to process information, analyze it, recall it at a later time, and draw conclusions from it, but "active listening" hears the *feelings* of the speaker first and processes information secondarily. Both deliberate and active listening skills are necessary in effective communication, but listening with feeling is far more important in marriage.

Active listening is particularly useful when you sense your mate has a problem—anger, resentment, loneliness, discouragement, frustration, hurt. Your first reaction to such feelings may be negative. You may want to argue, defend yourself, withdraw, or fight back. But in active listening you catch what has been said and then restate what you think the feeling is, not the facts of what has been said.

Carl: "Len Bradford, the new administrator, really gets my goat. He picks on the smallest things. He's always on my back. I don't know how much more I can take."

Helen, using active listening, says, "You mean Len Bradford is a very difficult person to work with," or "It's very difficult to work with someone who nit-picks." These responses allow Carl to feel that she understands the difficulty he faces at work. He has needed someone he could open up to about this problem, and now he feels free to express the full story. Helen listens with appropriate variations of active listening mixed with door openers and so provides the sounding board Carl needs. Sometimes it is necessary to prod gently to uncover the true emotion behind the words. When you think you understand, you then say it back, checking for any misunderstanding.

When Jan says, "I'm so tired I could die," Jack could say, "Stop talking about being tired and take some Geritol." Or, "You always get tired this time of night when you think I might

want more than a good-night kiss." But with active listening Jack would say, "You're really bushed, huh? Any special reason?" This now opens the door for Jan to seek understanding from her husband concerning certain problems she has had with the children, a run-in with a neighbor, or worries over her mother's health. She now knows Jack cares about her day and duties. It is easier for her to say more, go deeper into her problem, and develop her thoughts further. *Caution:* Once private feelings are exposed, however, you must restrain the urge to give advice, criticize, blame, or make judgments. *This is not the time for that.*

89

Rules for Effective Listening

Perhaps you have been a poor listener. Merely deciding to try to listen harder will not work. You must discipline yourself and make a firm commitment to improve this skill. Here are six ways you can practice listening with feeling on a daily basis.

1. Maintain good eye contact. Focus your full attention on your partner. (Turn off the television and put down the paper.)

2. Sit attentively. For a few minutes act as if nothing else in the world matters except hearing your partner out. Block all other distractions from your mind. Lean forward in your chair.

3. Act interested in what you are about to hear. Raise your eyebrows, nod your head, smile, or laugh when appropriate.

4. Sprinkle your attentive listening with appropriate phrases to show agreement, interest, and understanding. Your partner wants to know that you understand the ideas he's presenting. Try to think through what he is saying and fit it into your own experience.

5. Ask well-phrased questions. Give encouragement by asking questions that illustrate your interest.

6. Listen a little longer. Just when you think you are through listening, listen thirty seconds longer.

Do you have a communication problem? During the next week focus your attention not on your mate's failures but on your own. Being aware is only the first step. Next, set about to correct the problem. And last, follow through in an attempt to upgrade your communication with your loved ones. If you are uncertain whether a problem exists, ask your mate what he dislikes the most about the way you talk or listen.

Solving Conflicts

Conflicts in marriage are inevitable. Husbands and wives view things differently, and marriage would be very dull if they didn't. But out of these differences disagreements can arise, and from disagreements, conflicts arise that can result in highly emotional states of frustration and anger.

Often couples view conflict with horror, believing that it threatens their relationship. This misconception causes some to avoid conflict by refusing to acknowledge its presence, by running from it, and by forcing feelings underground. But ignoring conflicts does not solve them. In fact, serious problems sometimes develop when problems are bottled up inside and are not released. A few simple rules can lead to constructive problem-solving.

1 Choose the best time and place. It is best to keep current when handling conflicts, but if either of you is angry or unreasonable, then postpone the discussion. Don't delay it for too long, however. And if your partner does not bring up the issue again, then you take the initiative to solve the problem. Guard against unnecessary interruptions when discussing major issues. You may want to take the phone off the hook and agree not to answer the door. If children are not part of the discussion, explain that you have an important issue to settle and ask them not to disturb you. If you can handle the problem constructively, it is not detrimental to allow them to observe and thus learn healthy methods of handling disagreements.

Try not to discuss major issues late at night. Decisions made late in the day when the body is mentally, physically, and spiritually exhausted are likely to be emotional ones. A better plan would be to sleep on it overnight and arise an hour early.

Many well-organized families set aside a definite time each week as "gripe night." This eliminates unpleasant conversation during meals and at other inappropriate times while allowing for issues to be discussed before they get out of hand.

2 Say it straight. State your feelings openly and respectfully through the *effective* use of I-messages. Speak directly, clearly, and concisely without anger. Include reasons why you hold your opinion. Explain how you think the problem can be solved and what is at stake. Speak in as calm and controlled a manner as possible, lowering the volume of your voice rather than raising it.

3 Stay on the subject. Stick with one problem until you solve it. The more problems brought up at one time, the less likelihood that any of them will still respect his right to have his opinion. Here are some no-nos: no name-calling, no wild threats of divorce or suicide, no remarks about in-laws or relatives, no put-downs concerning appearance or intelligence, no physical violence, no yelling, and no interrupting.

Words spoken in anger can never be recalled. Nothing can erase the effect of a threatening ultimatum or bitter remarks spoken in anger. Speak and listen with respect.

5 List the solutions. When feelings have been described openly and constructively, you will see the issues at stake and work out rational alternatives. Brainstorm every possible solution regardless of how farfetched it may seem, but do not appraise them at this time.

6 Evaluate the solutions. Once all available information has been aired, the two of you can make an intelligent choice as to the course of action most likely to succeed. Go back through the list and share thoughts on the consequences as you evaluate each solution.

be solved. Make a rule that additional problems cannot be brought up until the first one has been dealt with. If necessary, prepare a sheet of paper titled "Agenda for Next Conference" and jot down other issues. Avoid dragging up old scores and arguments. Agree that if the accusation is over six months old, it is inadmissible evidence.

4 Show respect. You may not agree with your mate's position. You may be violently opposed. But you can

7 Choose the most acceptable solution. Commit yourselves to choosing the solution closest to meeting the needs of both of you or the needs of the one hurting the most. This choice may take a good measure of negotiation and compromise. Winning should not be the goal, because where there is a winner there must also be a loser, and no one likes to lose.

Solutions can be reached by one partner yielding, by both compromising, or by one giving in to the other rather than just giving in. Take care to see that one of you does not always do the yielding. It takes two to make a conflict and two to resolve it. Giving in to another in the midst of conflict takes real maturity, because in effect you are admitting that your analysis of the situation was wrong and that you are now ready to change your mind.

8 Implement the decision. Decide who is to do what, where, and when. Once you reach a decision, remember that two persons often perceive agreements differently. When this happens, try jotting down the specifications in an agreement book that each party signs. This technique is effective with children, too, especially teenagers.

Only friendly negotiation can solve some conflicts. Often if one gives in, the other feels resentful and may be in a very bad mood for the rest of the evening—refusing to speak, getting very little sleep, and carrying the argument through to the next day. The other mate can be just as stubborn. Each feels justified in supporting his or her own decision. But does it really matter who is right and who is wrong? A couple that cares about each other should be able to work things out according to how important each one considers his or her needs at the time. A solution can be reached easier when each person is willing to see the problem from the other's viewpoint.

When Your Partner Breaks the Rules

Try as you may to avoid arguments, at times you will be drawn into them. When you see one coming, you can prevent it by following a simple formula.

Rather than responding with words that throw you into the heat of battle, *choose not to argue.*

If your husband reads something hostile into a perfectly legitimate request, choose not to argue but state calmly and reasonably: "I'm sorry it sounded like that. What I meant to convey is that . . ."

If your mate has a special gift for sarcasm, tell him openly: "It hurts me to hear remarks like that about me. I know I do things that hurt you also, but let's try to avoid such things in the future."

If you live with a faultfinder, don't defend yourself. Instead, take notes on your "sins." When he has gotten it all off his chest, say something like this: "OK, let's go back to the first thing you mentioned. If I'm really at fault here, I'm willing to talk it over with you. I'll ask the same of you, too."

When a partner makes a ridiculous exaggeration, such as, "You never come home on time," rather than correcting the statement, try: "I know this upsets you and that you feel it happens too often. I'll try not to let it happen again."

If your husband breaks his agreement not to yell at you because you spend so much money, check your own

Active Listening Work Sheet

In order to help you form active listening responses a number of situations are listed below that require active listening skills. Read the problem and then write down an appropriate active listening response. Share your responses with your mate.

SOME HELPFUL PHRASES MIGHT BE . . .
You are feeling. . .
I see. You are saying . . .
You are really . . .
It's kind of like . . .
From what I'm hearing it seems you feel . . .
Let me see if I understand correctly . . .
So you are saying . . .
It sounds as if you are feeling . . .

The Problem

You might say

1. John voices uncertainty about staying with his present vocation.

2. Martha is upset over words she had with a neighbor.

3. Jim is angry because he just lost a big sale to a competitor.

4. Catherine is upset because she left a package in the department store after purchasing it.

5. Tony expresses frustration about a secretary at the office who is a nice girl but who just can't hack the work.

6. Mary complains that she can't keep up the house and the yard work both.

7. John expresses concern over financial problems.

8. Pam feels left out because she wasn't invited to a friend's party.

angry response and tell him that he has a good point and that you'll try to cut expenses in the future. Then, at another time, when he has calmed down, bring the budget up for discussion and work out a plan agreeable to both of you.

Unfair fighting techniques can destroy a relationship, but when your mate forgets and breaks the rules, *you can learn to stay reasonable.* Choose not to argue, but calmly and quietly confront your mate with the reality of the situation. With controlled aggression, reassert your own thoughts, feelings, and convictions. You can avoid many potential arguments by choosing not to argue and by responding in a reasonable, concerned, and tactful manner.

Intimate Communication

So far this chapter has presented better techniques for speaking, listening, and handling conflicts. But you could follow all these suggestions and still not really *know* your mate. The truth is that most husbands and wives don't know each other because many couples are very cautious about sharing their innermost thoughts and feelings with one another.

Studies show that communication peaks during the first year of marriage while a couple explore inner feelings and set goals for the future. But in a few years children enter the scene, and attention is diverted from husband and wife to home and children. Romance wears off, and the relationship takes on the appearance of a business partnership. Conversation centers on financial problems, the fight Tommy had at school, and Susie's poor grades.

In the meantime husband and wife have been pursuing different interests. He has been expanding his business ventures and protecting the family's fu-

ture. Her life has centered around her home, the children, and her hobbies. Within a few years the children leave the nest, and the couple in their middle years find that they have no basis for communication in depth.

Too many couples are sharing and communicating, but only about things—their jobs, the car, the house, the kids, the church. Is this how you communicated when you were courting each other? I doubt it. All you wanted then was to be together and to converse with one another. It hardly mattered what you did together, only that you were together. As you talked you frequently used the words *I, you, we, us.* You were not so concerned with things as you were to discover each other.

During all stages of married life, couples need a method whereby they can get in touch and stay in touch with the other partner's feelings. Perhaps you are aware that your communication has consisted mostly of exchanges of ideas, concepts, and hopes for the future, but you know little of how your mate feels inside.

"Talk back" is a plan whereby couples can regain the intimacy that was either lost or forgotten with the passing of time. This four-point pro-

Planning to Solve Problems

1. List ground rules (procedures).
   a.
   b.
   c.
   d.
   e.
2. Brainstorm solutions.
   a.
   b.
   c.
   d.
   e.

3. Evaluate suggestions.
   First choice:

   Second choice:

   Third choice:

4. Choose the best one *for all parties*.
5. Implement the choice.
   a. Method

   b. Action

gram involves choosing a subject for discussion. A choice is endless, but some suggestions are: My greatest emotional need is . . . , You can best fill my need for love by . . . , How I feel about our finances . . . , What I'd like to do with my free time . . . , How I feel about disciplining the children . . . , The happiest moment of my life with you was when . . . , I like you because. . . .

The subject is not as important as the sharing of feelings about it. After you have decided on a subject, reflect and write on it for just ten minutes. Writing is the key part but the most difficult task, yet it is essential if talk back is to work. Writing has several advantages over talking about feelings. It allows us to examine our thoughts and pay better attention to what we are saying. It also slows us down so that we can see our words and correct them if need be.

Style is not important. Don't worry if your thoughts seem insignificant or disconnected. The important thing is to get your feelings down on paper. Describe them, looking for feelings you haven't noticed before. Go deep inside yourself and describe what is there to the last detail. The aim is to aid your mate in experiencing how you feel, to help him see and understand as you see and un-derstand, to help him become a part of you for a time.

At some specified time during the day when the two of you can be alone, share what you have written with your mate, each of you reading silently what the other has written. After the initial reading, which acquaints you with the facts, read it again for feelings. Absorb all the hidden emotions and meanings expressed. Wife, try to feel as he feels. Husband, see as she sees, understand as she understands.

Now take turns responding to what has been written. Ask your mate to tell you more about how he feels. Describe to him how you perceive what he feels, and feed him ways of further expressing himself. Be physically close enough to experience as much as possible about what the other is feeling. Be sensitive to facial expressions, tears, sweaty or cold hands, or goose bumps on the arms. It is one thing to see a tear fall from your mate's eye and another to *feel* it fall. Communicate through the avenue of touch.

Practice talk-back daily for three months. At first this may sound like another job to be fitted into an already overcrowded schedule. But *daily* is the key word, for it isn't the once-in-a-lifetime heroic act that counts as much as daily actions. The flawless rendition of a concert musician comes as a result of daily practice. The ice skater, the gymnast, or anyone who does a job well owes his success to practice. Similarly, the couple who practice talk-back regularly will reap the greatest rewards from their relationship.

Although this chapter has centered on communication between husband and wife, it would not be complete without mentioning communication with God. Husband, wife, and God form a holy triangle. If communication breaks down between husband and wife, it affects their relationship with God. If the circuits are jammed toward heaven, there will be a busy signal between the couple too. One author has said, "A person cannot be genuinely open to God and closed to his mate." When the lines of communication are in working order, God can more easily fulfill His purpose for husband and wife.

No amount of expert communication will make a perfect marriage or create openness and respect where these qualities are not already present. But honest communication does relieve emotional tension, clarify thinking, and provide a release for daily pressures. It allows a couple to work toward common goals and paves the way toward a truly intimate relationship between husband and wife and God.

Further reading you will enjoy...

Augsburger, David. *CARING ENOUGH TO CONFRONT.*
Mayhall, Jack. *MARRIAGE TAKES MORE THAN LOVE.*
Salz, Victor. *BETWEEN HUSBAND AND WIFE.*
Small, Dwight. *AFTER YOU'VE SAID I DO.*
Umphrey, Marjorie. *GETTING TO KNOW YOU.*
Wahlroos, Sven. *FAMILY COMMUNICATION.*
Wright, Norman. *COMMUNICATION: KEY TO YOUR MARRIAGE.*

Part of what annoys us in marriage is individual characteristics due to sex. We need to understand that there are differences between the sexes that cannot be given up or even materially changed. Much of what irritates us has been classed as "faults," when actually it is little more than a created difference. Once this fact is understood, we need not be so prone to suspect the other of deliberate irritation. These things can then be accepted much like a natural phenomenon that may not be pleasant, but something that cannot be changed through any amount of scolding or nagging.

Chapter at a Glance

I. What Men Need to Know About Women

A. A woman's need for self-respect
   1. A lack of self-respect can
      a. be passed on to children
      b. affect her feelings of femininity
      c. produce negative feelings toward herself
      d. affect her homemaking
   2. She needs respect, appreciation, and interest in the way she meets her daily responsibilities

B. Outside interests
   1. She needs an afternoon or evening away from home
   2. Especially true for mothers of small children
   3. A necessity for her sanity and self-respect

C. Hired help
D. More communication
E. Time for family
F. Interest in the home
G. Feelings validated

Understand Your Mate

Every cell of the male differs genetically from any cell in the female. As a result of these genetic differences, females generally possess greater physical vitality. Thus, the average U.S. woman outlives the typical man by three to four years—perhaps because females tend to have a lower basal metabolism than that of males. The female skeletal structure also differs from the male—the female having a shorter head and legs, broader face, a less protruding chin, and a longer trunk. Women seem to lose their teeth earlier than do men. The stomach, kidneys, liver, and appendix are larger in females, but their lungs are smaller.

The thyroid gland, larger and more active in the female than the male, enlarges even further during pregnancy and menstruation, making females more prone to goiter problems. The larger thyroid provides the female with those elements that we consider important to personal beauty, such as smooth skin, a relatively hair-free body, and a thin layer of subcutaneous fat.

Female blood contains more water and 20 percent fewer red cells. Since these red cells supply oxygen to the

---

H. Woman's intuition
I. Mood changes
J. Premenstrual changes
K. Attention

II. What Women Need to Know About Men
  A. Masculine identity
    1. Male proud of masculinity
    2. Vulnerable to criticism
    3. May invent cover-ups to hide weaknesses
    4. Longs for a "safe" relationship
  B. Outside relationships

  C. Male goals
    1. Vocation comes first
    2. Also seeks status and position
  D. Be nice to come home to
    1. Prepare mood
    2. Prepare physical self
    3. Make home atmosphere pleasant
  E. Discouraged husbands
    1. Moodiness, depression, discouragement, common because of business pressures
    2. Doesn't need someone with solutions

body, this may explain why women may tire more easily and are more apt to faint. During World War II when the workday in British wartime factories was increased from ten to twelve hours a day, accidents among women rose 150 percent, but the accident rate among men remained unaffected. However, whereas women may tire more easily in a given day, they have the capacity to live more days.

Menstruation, pregnancy, and lactation affect female behavior and emotions. Research into suicides shows that 40 to 60 percent of the women were menstruating when they took their own lives. David Levy found that the depth and intensity of the maternal instinct is associated with the duration and amount of the menstrual flow.

The increased glandular activity during menstruation produces marked changes in female behavior. Studies of behavior change show a large portion of women's crimes (63 percent in an English study and 84 percent in a French) occurred just prior to the onset of menstruation. Suicides, accidents, a decline in quality in academic attainment and intelligence test scores, and visual clarity and response speed were also markedly affected by menstrua-

tion. Absenteeism due to menstrual problems costs the United States about five million dollars annually, but the financial toll is secondary to the repercussions in the home resulting from domestic quarrels during this time.

Some of these differences, whether they are innate or acquired, can cause many misunderstandings if we insist on thinking like our sex but deny our mates the privilege to think as do their sex. Trouble begins when either sex becomes dogmatic in thinking his or her views alone are "right."

We do not want to oversimplify matters, and it is difficult to lump all males or all females into one basket and assume that each will always respond in accordance with his or her sex. We cannot assume that everyone of the same sex will always have identical emotional needs or duplicate behavior patterns or precisely corresponding ways of thinking. But by studying general trends within each sex, we can gain insights into how the other half will often think and respond.

What Men Need to Know About Women

Until recently, few authorities even attempted to clarify the female personality. Instead, many people viewed women as a complicated mixture of conflicting, unrealistic, illogical needs that were difficult, if not impossible, to supply. Women may appear to be more complicated on the surface, but this is mostly because they operate on a different wavelength than do men and consequently approach life from another angle. Someone has said that every once in a while a man gets a flash of insight into what makes his wife tick, and just as he is pondering this . . . she tocks!

A Woman's Need for Self-respect

In a survey conducted by Dr. James Dobson on the sources of depression in women, they listed low self-esteem as their most troubling problem. He observed that even in seemingly healthy and happily married young women, personal inferiority and self-doubt hurt the most and left the most wicked scars.

Why are women suffering from depression due to feelings of low self-worth? The answer, at least in part, lies with the fact that the female role is under fire today. Women are told that if they devote themselves to homemaking they are worthless. More and more a woman's worth is measured only in terms of her financial asset to the family and her contribution to the business world. Buffeted on every side by radio, television, magazines, newspapers, and movies, she begins to assume that if she isn't a super or bionic woman, a news reporter, a physician, or policewoman, she is nothing. These options should be open for women today, but not at the expense of disparaging the role of wife, mother, and homemaker or of destroying self-esteem.

A mother's lack of self-respect will affect the home in many ways. First of all, she will pass it on to the children. They will see that she does not respect herself, and they will not respect her either and will unconsciously pick up tendencies toward a negative self-concept of themselves. It is impossible for a mother with a poor self-image to pass on to her children a healthy concept of themselves, and they will always be lacking in this area unless someone else with a good self-image heavily compensates for their lack.

Second, a low self-concept will affect a woman's femininity. If she doesn't have positive feelings about herself, she will most likely not enjoy being a female. Negative attitudes will take over. She may lament her lot in life, complain endlessly, and fight against adapting herself to her husband's wishes. It is a psychological truth that we cannot love others until we love ourselves first, and a wife can love her husband only in direct proportion to how well she feels about herself.

Third, such negative feelings will affect the sex life. If a woman doesn't have positive feelings about being female or doesn't like the way she looks, she will not understand her hus-

Carefully and Prayerfully Read the Following Texts

"Share each other's troubles and problems, and so obey our Lord's command" (Galatians 6:2, TLB).

"When others are happy, be happy with them. If they are sad, share their sorrow. Work happily together" (Romans 12:15, 16, TLB).

In what specific and practical ways can you see yourself putting this advice to use in better understanding your mate? Be as specific as your feeling will allow.

When will you begin to do this? What results might you expect from this plan of action?

band's sexual desires toward her. She may wear high-necked, long flannel nightgowns in an effort to hide what she considers a disgusting body. She may insist on undressing in the bathroom or making love in total darkness—calculated attempts to forget that she has a woman's body.

Fourth, a low self-concept affects one's homemaking ability. Especially if a wife has attended college, she may begin to belittle herself because society is beginning to belittle homemaking. Guilt feelings may consume her because she always seems to stay behind in her work. She can scrub and clean all day and have the house spotless when hubby returns home, yet never feel satisfied with her efforts. She exhausts herself in pursuing endless tasks in an effort to prove that she has some worth.

Little wonder that a woman needs respect from her husband for the way she meets her daily responsibilities. A man gains this respect through job promotions, pay raises, annual evaluations, bonuses, and praise. But a homemaker has no one from whom to get such encouragement except from her husband. The unhappiest women in the world are those who must drag through day after weary day with no understanding from their husbands of what it takes to run a home and to raise responsible children.

Outside Interests

A man who really wants to do something positive to build self-respect in his wife should see to it that she gets out of the house and away from the children at least one afternoon or day a week. This is particularly true for mothers of small children.

A homemaker who can get out of the house one day a week for a luncheon with the girls or a self-improvement or hobby class will be a better wife and mother. And she will enjoy her homemaking more because of the new slant on life that she brings back into the home. If finances are tight, she can exchange baby-sitting with a neighbor or friend. This is not a convenience to be worked into the budget if there are reserve funds, but a *must* for keeping her sanity and self-respect.

Hired Help

A man might also check into a little hired help with the big jobs—washing the windows, stripping and waxing floors, shampooing carpets. This, of course, would be expensive if done through a professional agency, but many high school girls are eager to make some spending money. Such a program has many rewards, not the least of which is a less-fatigued wife at night.

More Communication

A man who wants his wife to accept the responsibilities of motherhood and to supply the children with a nurturing love and a positive self-image should provide the support she needs. If she has had an especially difficult day solving the hundreds of little crises that come up hourly in the realm of raising children, then he must allow her time to talk with him about these problems that are important to her. She needs his help to discipline, train, guide, entertain, and educate the children.

Time for the Family

Every man should reserve some time in his busy work schedule for his family. If his job particularly rewards many of his ego needs and if he loves what he is doing, it might not be hard for him to invest six or almost seven days a week in his occupation. The result is a frustrated wife and lonesome children.

A minister friend of ours always took time for his wife and family. He pastored a large church in a huge metropolis and, had he allowed it, could have ministered to the flock 100 percent of his waking hours. But he wouldn't let this happen; so he spent every Monday with his family. Often they would leave home and go off by themselves. If they did stay home, they refused to answer the phone. Only his secretary knew how to reach him in an emergency. He had his priorities

straight. After all, what good would his position and his church be to him if he lost the admiration and affection of his own family? He has succeeded as a pastor, husband, and father because he has kept his values in order.

Interest in the Home

If a man spends most of his time away from the home and if he fails to manifest equal interest in what goes on in the home, his wife will feel frustrated. Home is an extension of her personality, and she may interpret his attitude as personal unconcern for her. For example, he may not be handy at puttering around the house. Attempting to repair the leaky faucet, sagging towel rack, and one-hinged screen door may frustrate him and seem minor compared to the more important matters on his mind. "What does it matter if these things get done now or a month from now?" he asks himself. But to her his procrastination may represent personal rejection. She needs to know he cares about her world and her.

Although a woman needs her husband's participation and interest in the home, he must remember that it is *her* domain. Even if he is an efficiency expert, he should not try to rearrange her kitchen or redecorate the house alone. This would be as bad as if she went to his office and rearranged the furniture, gave counterinstructions to his secretary, and showed him where he was wrong in many of his decisions. A woman needs freedom in choosing house plans and decor. It is her world.

Validate Feelings

A woman needs to have her feelings validated and accepted. She does not look primarily for solutions so much as for understanding. She will be satisfied to seek for a solution later, but when she is upset she wants adult conversation. If a man listens with one ear or if he appears uninterested, it will not be good enough. So she may provoke an argument by choosing an insignificant point and blowing it all out of proportion.

Carl G. Jung speaks of the tendency for an intellectual woman to harp on an irrelevant point, nonsensically making it the main one. He points out that a perfectly lucid discussion can often get tangled up in the most maddening way through the introduction of different and sometimes perverse points of view. She may drag up five-year-old inconsequentials and leap to wild conclusions. Usually during such episodes she does not really want an argument. She only wants her husband to understand how she feels. In most cases she does not wish to win the argument, and would be disappointed if she did.

Respect Intuition

A man sometimes feels that a woman cannot be understood because she approaches problem-solving differently. A man relies heavily on pure logic for understanding, whereas a woman does not normally analyze a situation, reduce it into component parts, and produce a factual solution. She usually perceives by an emotional process.

A man tends to disregard the emotional reactions of a woman because they lack substance according to male standards. But a mature woman can produce highly accurate conclusions. Feminine intuition, as it is often called, can greatly benefit a man by lending a broader perspective to an issue. Men—and sometimes women—tend to put down what can be a valuable resource, for intuition is not magical thinking but rather ideas, perceptions, thoughts, and feelings that emerge from a woman's reflection on issues. She may have limited knowledge of a subject, but her advice can prove quite reliable.

A lawyer once said, "Half my male clients would have kept out of trouble if they had talked things over with their wives. I suppose it isn't my place to tell them so, but I can't understand how an intelligent man, who has an intelligent wife, fails to use her more profitably. Why should he want to let half of his capital stock lie idle? Even if his own judgment is unusually good, he gets so close to a deal that he can't see the forest for the trees. If he would talk it

My Needs

Women, complete these sentences:

1. When I feel like crying, I want my husband to . . .

2. I love my husband when he shows personal interest in and attention to me by . . .

3. My husband could better fill my need for communication on a more personal level by . . .

4. I love my husband when he builds my self-respect by . . .

5. I'd like my husband to build my self-respect more by . . .

6. My husband treats my woman's intuition . . .

7. When I am experiencing menstrual or premenstrual tension, I like my husband to . . .

8. I'd like my husband to show more interest in our home by . . .

9. My needs for a creative outlet outside the home could be filled by . . .

over with his wife, who may know nothing about it, she would yet aid him in seeing the outlines clearly by the very fact that her mind is free and untrammeled. Men come to me for just that sort of a service and pay me large fees. Half the time their wives could do the job as well as I, since it doesn't call for any legal knowledge—merely common sense and a detached mind that looks at the matter freshly.''

Mood Changes

A woman often experiences volatile mood swings, which a man may interpret as emotional unstability. But the ups and downs a woman experiences result from her entirely different emotional setup and glandular changes.

One aspect of a woman's emotional nature that can greatly frustrate a man is her crying spells. Sometimes a woman cries over a major issue, and sometimes it seems minor. She can cry on schedule or off. These spells do not show a lack of discipline, however, but rather her sensitive nature. She may cry as a release from pent-up tension, or she may cry when she is deeply touched, hurt, or happy. During such times most women

would appreciate a tender expression of sympathy indicating that their emotions are understood. Others may wish to shed their tears undisturbed. In most cases, a good cry represents "therapy."

Premenstrual Tension

Men should try to understand the psychological factors that occur during premenstrual tension and anticipate likely emotional changes. About five days prior to menstruation, the estrogen content of the bloodstream is elevated, which causes the body to retain fluid. In some cases it can amount to as much as five excess pounds. This bloated condition, in addition to the newly released hormones, often results in sluggishness, depression, and tension as well as cramps.

Many marital problems erupt just prior to menstruation, and a wife will particularly need affection and reassurance during this time, even though she may be at her most unlovable worst. It is best not to decide important family issues at this time. If the wife can be aware that she is uptight, she can make allowances for her behavior, and her husband can too. He should do all he can to keep the house running as smoothly as possible.

Not Things—but Attention

Today's society places a great amount of emphasis upon the acquisition of things. As a consequence, men have heart attacks at earlier ages due to excessive stress. Yet few women really want more things, for things can never take the place of a loving husband.

At some point in his life every man must face the reality that time is passing, that his life is vanishing right before his eyes. Wedding anniversaries have come and gone, and the years have disappeared. The children will soon be gone, and the husband may discover that he is living with a stranger whom he calls his wife. If this is how it is with you, perhaps you need to assess what is really worth your time and effort. What do you wish to recall at the end of your days? If you aren't after wealth and fame, what is it you want? Unless you have experienced the warmth of family ties, service to others, and a sincere attempt to serve God, nothing else will make much sense, will it?

What Women Need to Know About Men

On numerous occasions I have questioned the ladies attending my Fulfilled Womanhood seminars about what brought them to the classes. I have done this so that I might better present material that will meet their needs and also to increase the effectiveness of my advertising. The overwhelming answer has typically been their desire to understand men better. Since the first ten hours of the twelve-hour seminar deal with specific aspects of understanding the male temperament more fully, the women were always pleased.

Although all men are not alike, what is said here can help a wife understand that her husband is normal when he exhibits certain attitudes, actions, and tendencies that are basically male.

Masculine Identity

Just as each cell of a woman's body genetically differs from those of a man, every cell of a man's body forever sets him apart as a male. He is proud of being male and of all those characteristics that distinguish him from his female counterpart. Indeed, if he feels that he

A Quick Look at Priorities

According to the way you are presently living, put the following list in order of priority. No. 1 has the highest priority. You may add to the list.

Mate
Hobbies
Children
God
Work outside the home
Home responsibilities
Church
Job
Recreation
Social activities
Sports
Material goods

Now rearrange the priorities as you would like to have them. What are the significant differences between the two lists? Are there areas that need to be changed? If so, list them.

What steps are you willing to take in order to make changes?

lacks any essential male qualities, he may well invent a number of cover-ups in order to hide the fact from the world as well as from his wife. Some might include ruling with an iron fist, sarcasm, ironic humor, tough talk, highly rational and logical arguments, or stinginess. Even those closest to him may not be able to see through the cover-ups he has invented to protect himself.

Have you ever made a strictly casual remark to your husband to which he responded sharply? Or maybe he withdrew into a period of silence? "Now

what did I say wrong?" you wonder in exasperation. Unknowingly you probably touched a sensitive spot.

Most of the time wives do not deliberately attack their husbands with cruel remarks just to hurt them. More often they do it innocently or thoughtlessly, but comments such as "You call that being a man?" or "Why don't you grow up?" or "Can't you show some leadership?" or "You and your balding charms!" are all cutting jibes aimed not only at bringing a man down to size but also at alienating him.

One woman almost wrecked her husband's career by making fun of him. He started out as a salesman for a product that he liked and was enthusiastic about. But when he came home at night, hungry for a little encouragement, she would greet him by saying, "Well, how's the boy genius tonight? Did you bring home any commissions, or just a lecture or two from the sales manager? I suppose you know the house payment is due next week?" She carried on like this for years, but despite her constant sneers, he forged ahead by sheer ability.

Today he is an executive vice-president in a nationally known concern. His wife? He divorced her and married another woman who gives him all the affectionate support his first wife denied him. And wife No. 1 can't understand why she lost her husband. "After all my years of scrimping and saving," she moans to her friends, "Jerry left me for a younger woman when he didn't need me to slave for him any longer. That's a man for you!"

She did not seem to recognize that every man longs for a relationship so private and intimate that he can let his guard down and release his pent-up feelings freely and safely. He dreams of this kind of intimacy and is keenly disappointed if he cannot find it. He wants

"Martha, my secretary doesn't understand me."

Drawing by Whitney Darrow, Jr., © 1939, 1967, The New Yorker Magazine, Inc.

to confide secrets of his inner self, things that he shares with no one else.

A Reach Outside the Relationship

When a man experiences a sense of fulfillment and joy, he usually wishes to reach outside the marital relationship—kidding with waitresses, inviting friends over, throwing a celebration, or initiating big plans for his work. He is not really avoiding or depreciating his marital relationship but is, instead, figuratively speaking "beating his chest." Such behavior comes out in very different ways according to the particular personality, but a quality of "look at me" is in it all. Because women typically like to savor the warmth of happy moments and quietly relive the experience over and over, they often feel embarrassed or threatened by this aspect of the male personality. But this reaching out to others is another aspect of maleness.

Closely connected to the "reaching out" process is a man's need for companions and interests outside the home. Usually such pursuits will make him a better husband and strengthen his self-thinks that her husband works so hard just to make more money, but in most cases this isn't true. Most men need this feeling of competing and succeeding to fulfill their basic male needs. A man can better fill his wife's needs and feel happier and more romantic when he thinks of himself as a success.

Some women fight their husband's decision to invest, to expand in business, to change occupations, to move to another city. *Woman's Day* magazine interviewed famous men's wives to see what part they had played in the success of their husbands.

Elizabeth Fulbright, wife of the Arkansas senator, spoke for many of the wives when she said, " 'If a man isn't happy in what he's doing, his wife can't be happy either.' Once you realize this, it's a lot easier to go along with a change of careers, even a risky one."

Senator George McGovern, for instance, had already changed careers twice before he went into politics. " 'The odds were against him the first time he ran,' " said his wife, Eleanor. " 'Everyone told him so, but he won anyway. I'm so glad I didn't say "don't." ' "

image and feelings of individuality because it breaks his monotony and also gives him a place to drain off discouragement and discontent. A wife should allow her husband to have his male interests and hobbies without making him feel guilty. Some women fight their husbands on this, but even when they win, they lose, for a dominated husband's greatest wish is usually to escape.

Male Goals

Sometimes a woman fails to understand a man's priorities in life—that he must put his work ahead of her at times if he is to succeed. The burdens and strains of today's business world put a man under tremendous pressure. As a consequence, men have over ten times more accidental deaths, suicides, and mental breakdowns than do women. But a woman rarely understands how heavily the burden weighs upon a man to earn a living, to succeed at an occupation, and to get ahead in the world, for men rarely speak about it. They do not want to worry their loved ones.

A man also has a built-in drive for position and status that most women fail to understand. A wife often mistakenly

Be Nice to Come Home To

Dr. Anna K. Daniels, a marriage counselor and author, says simply, "Being nice to come home to is the finest thing a woman can do." "Even if I have to let other things go," a wife told me once, "I always find time for a relaxing shower and a quick change into something pretty before my husband comes home. I know my mood is more important than anything else." Good advice. A woman who freshens her makeup and hair and changes into something feminine will have a husband who will look forward to coming home evenings.

Most men enjoy a period of quiet

My Needs

Men, complete these sentences:

1. I wish my wife understood my need for . . .

2. My wife could make our place pleasant to come home to by . . .

3. When I become discouraged over business pressures, I like my wife to . . .

4. When I come home from work, I wish my wife would meet me looking like . . .

5. My wife builds my masculine identity by . . .

6. I feel uncomfortable when my wife cuts me down by . . .

7. My wife could lessen the pressure I'm under by . . .

8. I'd like it if my wife supported my interests outside the home by . . .

9. I wish my wife would show more interest in . . .

after a hard day. When there are small children about, it is difficult to manage this, but they can have their toys picked up and their hands and faces washed. Having very young children fed before Daddy comes home will eliminate their fussiness, and older children can do their homework when Dad is due home.

And when you meet him at the door, don't tell him right off about the fender you dented or the calls from the bill collectors. A man can better handle the day's disasters after a time of relaxation. If you detect that he's had an especially bad day, it might be best to put off unpleasant news till another time, if possible.

His Haven

A man needs the solitude of his haven in order to pull the tattered edges of his soul together again. Oh, it hardly matters if the tables are polished or if a decorator has chosen the decor, but rather what means so much is the atmosphere of the home—the degree of restfulness and warmth it offers. The wife knows that the colors, lighting, and furnishings of a home can spell the difference between a relaxed or a tensed-up husband. She recognizes that a little soft music can release tension, allay fears, alleviate boredom, and help digestion.

Discouraged Husbands

The pressures of earning a living sometimes make a man next to impossible to live with. Moodiness, depression, and discouragement are common among men battling the forces of the business world. However, a woman is in a position to give moral support to her husband during these periods of discouragement, but most don't know

how. I certainly didn't. Whenever Harry would come home beat and begin to tell his problems, I would listen carefully, *but* as soon as he finished I would launch all *my solutions!* I even felt puzzled and upset when he didn't receive my suggestions with enthusiasm.

I did not realize at that time that what a man wants when he experiences a problem is an understanding ear, not someone with all the answers. He wants someone he can open up to without interruption, someone who will listen attentively and empathetically. A wife with all the answers makes her husband

114

feel uncomfortable, inferior, and unnecessary.

If your husband is experiencing a problem and wants to talk with you about it, supply him with warmth and tenderness. Your attitude of understanding and listening will let him know you care. If he doesn't choose to tell you of his trouble, don't try to force the issue. He may be trying to hide certain failures from you. If he remains discouraged for a while, accept it. Give him as much time as he needs to get over his problem, and build him up through appreciation, approval, and belief in his abilities.

"If you ever lost faith in me, I'd be finished," a man told his wife recently. "But as long as you believe in me," he added, "I can lick the world." Believing in your husband is often easier than showing it. But more than anything else a man wants a wife who will understand him. She doesn't have to grasp all the intricacies of the problem but merely to lend a sympathetic ear to his needs of the moment. The wife who can listen to her husband's problems, share his concerns and successes, and contribute to

his self-confidence will also share deeply in his affections.

Seek to Understand

Francis of Assisi prayed, "Lord! Grant that I seek more to . . . understand than to be understood." This purpose in a marriage, quickened by the softening influence of the Holy Spirit, could completely transform a couple's misunderstandings. Otherwise, when one becomes preoccupied with merely being understood by his mate, he becomes selfish, demanding, and bitter.

Paul Tournier, a well-known Christian psychiatrist, feels so strongly about the need for mutual understanding between marital partners that he says husband and wife should become preoccupied with it—lost in it—engrossed to the fullest in learning what makes the other tick, what the other likes, dislikes, fears, worries about, dreams of, believes in, and *why* he or she feels that way. Such a purpose would lead a couple directly into the benefits of a most meaningful marriage.

Further reading you will enjoy...

Andelin, Helen. *FASCINATING WOMANHOOD,* chapters 5 and 6.
Benson, Dan. *THE TOTAL MAN,* Chapter 11.
Carnegie, Dorothy. *HOW TO HELP YOUR HUSBAND GET AHEAD.*
Dobson, James. *WHAT WIVES WISH THEIR HUSBANDS KNEW ABOUT WOMEN.*
Hardisty, Margaret. *FOREVER MY LOVE.*
Landorf, Joyce. *TOUGH AND TENDER.*
Lees, Hannah. *HELP YOUR HUSBAND STAY ALIVE.*
Mayhall, Jack. *MARRIAGE TAKES MORE THAN LOVE.*
Osborne, Cecil. *THE ART OF UNDERSTANDING YOUR MATE.*
Renich, Jill. *TO HAVE AND TO HOLD.*
Tournier, Paul. *TO UNDERSTAND EACH OTHER.*

*"Marriage is that relation
between man and woman
in which the independence is equal,
the dependence mutual,
and the obligation reciprocal."*
—L. K. Anspacher.

T Adams

Chapter at a Glance

I. Roles in Marriage

    A. Role patterns

        1. Patriarchal

        2. Matriarchal

        3. Co-leadership

        4. Power struggle

    B. The missing link

II. Mutual Submission

    A. Each partner submits to the other at times

    B. Each partner recognizes individual competencies

C. Each partner willing to adapt during conflict

D. Both are equal partners

E. Both give and take

III. The Supportive Relationship

    A. Definition

        1. Based on mutual submission

        2. Both partners give up power and control

        3. Both are willing to negotiate and adjust differences

        4. Husband will lead in some areas because of individual competence

Support Your Mate

After the groom has carried his bride over the threshold, questions arise about who should do what. Who will do the cooking and housework? Should she hold a job outside the home? If she does, will he help with the meals, the housecleaning, and the children? Since she has almost as much earning power as he, should he still make all the decisions for the family?

It was much simpler in Grandpa's day. After he carried his bride over the threshold, she dutifully trotted off to the kitchen, or wherever, and cheerfully (?) performed her tasks of scrubbing, washing, sewing, baking, and rearing children. Meanwhile her husband plowed the ground, milked the cows, and generally earned the living. Roles were simply and clearly defined.

But not so today. Increased advantages for women have liberated them from the kitchen and offered opportunities for competing with men. The trend for marriage is away from the patriarchal system (in which the man is head of the family and his word is law) or the semipatriarchal approach (in which his word is law most of the time). Today's approach tends more toward

5. Wife will lead in some areas because of individual competence
B. The supportive husband—
   1. understands wife's position
   2. offers supportive leadership
   3. sees problem areas
   4. takes spiritual leadership
   5. provides protective leadership
C. The supportive wife
   1. Submission is not—
      a. being a doormat
      b. helpless dependency
      c. servility
      d. blind obedience
   2. Submission is willingness to adapt one's rights to those of another
   3. Difficult situations
      a. An unworthy husband
      b. The weak leader
      c. The non-Christian husband
D. The benefits of a supportive relationship

an egalitarian relationship.

In the face of such changing attitudes, many Christian couples feel confused and wonder how to relate to the traditional roles of past generations and to the family patterns mentioned in Scripture.

Role Patterns

Roles, as a set of social obligations that husband and wife utilize in their interaction with each other, lend order, continuity, and predictability to marriage. Studies reveal, however, that few couples are aware of their role performance. Yet the inability or failure to carry out a role can cause marital tension and may even prove disastrous to marriage.

Four basic role patterns exist in Western culture today:

1. *Patriarchal.* In a patriarchal relationship the husband's leadership is unquestioned. His word is law. He determines all policies and rules for the entire family. There is ample Biblical support, particularly in the Old Testament, for anyone who wants to take this position. God said of Abraham, "I know him, that he will command his children and his household after him" (Genesis 18:19). The patriarchal leader may or may not choose to consult with family members, depending on his degree of authoritarianism.

2. *Matriarchal.* In a matriarchy the wife assumes the lead role as head of the family. It is not uncommon in other cultures, where it has met the society's needs for many years. In our Western culture it can sometimes happen by default when, for example, the husband may fail to direct the family or make decisions. Or the female may have usurped his authority.

3. *Coleadership.* This relatively new term has arisen as an outgrowth of the women's liberation movement. Here both husband and wife attempt to guide the family as two persons with equal authority and control. The decision of either party carries as much weight as the other's.

4. *Power struggle.* In this pattern both husband and wife compete for the leadership role. He fights against her when she attempts to make a decision, and she counters with methods of usurping his authority. The contestants have never clarified their rules, and authority in the family shifts from one partner to the other, depending on who wins the latest battle.

Perhaps by now you wonder, "Is this all there is to choose from?" No.

The Missing Link

All the sermons, marriage seminars, and books I've researched on the topic of roles in marriage seem to begin with verse 22 of Ephesians 5: "Wives, be subject to your husbands, as to the Lord" (RSV). Few, if any, authorities explain *how* to submit, *when* to submit, and whether the wife must submit to *everything*, or how to handle submis-sion when the husband does not profess Christianity.

Current emphasis on family life has caused some individuals to read further in Ephesians, and they have revived the apostolic counsel of Ephesians 5:25: "Husbands, love your wives, as Christ loved the church" (RSV). This additional information begins to balance what at first *seems* like an uneven scale. Even then a husband may ask, *how* should I love, *when* should I love, and *what attitudes* must I manifest in loving my wife?

Roles Are Important

Roles are the parts people choose in life. They become conventional ways of behaving. In themselves roles are neither good nor bad. Some roles are clear-cut. Others are not so clear.

Outline some role expectations you had for your partner:

1. Before marriage. . .

2. After marriage . . .

3. Now . . .

Now outline some role expectations you had for yourself:

1. Before marriage . . .

2. After marriage . . .

3. Now . . .

ject of roles. It is not a matter of submission and domination. It is not a master-slave relationship or a dictator-robot obedience but a relationship of *mutual submission.*

The Meaning of Mutual Submission

Before defining *mutual submission,* a definition of *submission* is in order. The word *submit* possesses strong emotional overtones in today's society—overtones such as groveling, losing one's identity, servility, blind obedience, and passivity. But it does not have to mean that. Instead, submission is a willingness on the part of one to adapt his or her own rights to those of the other. According to the New Testament, submission is the core of every Christian relationship. It is modeled after Christ's willing submission to His Father. He was never compelled to obey, but rather He voluntarily complied.

The term *"mutual submission,"* then, implies that the marriage relationship is not as one-sided as many have imagined it through the centuries. It does not mean that the husband always commands and that the wife always submits, for such an interpretation of the Scriptures leaves out the mutuality described in Ephesians 5:21, which applies just as much to the marriage relationship as it does to brothers and sisters in the faith. Mutual submission means that there are times when each partner defers to the other. Mutual submission recognizes individual competencies. Each partner also operates with a willingness to adapt during times of conflict. Obviously mutual submission can function only when both partners consider each other as equals. Domination, not submission, occurs when an inferior surrenders to a

But one principle still remains overlooked. Preceding "Wives, submit . . ." and "Husbands, love . . ." the author of Ephesians puts both of these principles in proper perspective, and yet it almost *always* remains unmentioned. Verse 21 of Ephesians 5 reads: "Be subject to one another out of reverence for Christ" (RSV). It is the great principle undergirding all Christian relationships, and it is reinforced by such texts as "Submit yourselves to every ordinance of man" (1 Peter 2:13) and "Bear one another's burdens" (Galatians 6:2).

Here is the missing link in the subsuperior person. I see the supreme example of mutual submission in the relationship of God the Father and Jesus. Jesus was perfectly submissive to the will of His Father, but the fact that He submitted did not alter His status of equality. Couples should aim for this type of relationship.

Marriage requires a good deal of mutual submission, or in other words, give and take. Harry and I have certainly learned it. He prefers classical music, and I am strictly a semiclassical fan. Therefore he plays his heavy favorites when I'm not around. I'm an early-to-bed, early-to-rise person. He's a night owl. He's a pessimist. I'm the eternal optimist. He's a spender. I'm a saver. He's relaxed and easygoing. I'm an efficiency expert. Without mutual submission these differences in personality would be nearly impossible to work out.

Each of the four previous role patterns listed leaves something to be desired for today's Christian society. The heavy-handed, commanding, dictatorial, head-of-house system is outmoded in these times of equality and liberation. It can leave the wife feeling like something less than a person, and the accompanying results are destructive for both husband and wife as individuals as well as for the marriage itself.

The matriarchal system sometimes sets the stage for many social problems, not the least of which may be homosexuality. "The rise of homosexuality among our youth is one of the major failures of American home life. . . . There was a time when people tended to believe the homosexual was born that way. . . . Now it is generally agreed that . . . [it] is a result of childhood experience, often fomented by a too-doting mother and a disinterested or negligent father" (David Wilkerson, *Parents on Trial,* pp. 115, 116). Now,

the causes of homosexuality are complex, and the possibility exists that we have not yet identified all the causes, but certainly a strong mother figure and a weak father figure can be contributing factors.

Even the most progressive couple who attempt to function as coleaders encounter a multitude of frustrations in the area of problem-solving. Harry and I are bicycle enthusiasts. Particularly during warm spring evenings before the Fresno heat descends upon us, we enjoy nightly rides together. One night

Role-Expectation Exercise

Partners are to complete the role-expectation exercise individually. In the first column are listed a number of family functions. In the second column indicate who you think should do it in your family. (Use the following key: H—Husband; W—Wife; BH—Both, but husband more than wife; BW—Both, but wife more than husband; BE—Both equally.) In the third column you are to write who actually performs the function in your family. In the fourth and fifth columns briefly indicate the criteria and their sources for your decision. Move quickly through the items. Don't spend too much time on any one. First impressions will do. If an item doesn't apply, move on.

	WHO SHOULD HAVE THE RESONSI-BILITY?	WHO DOES IT IN YOUR RE-LATIONSHIP?	WHAT CRITERIA DID YOU USE TO DETERMINE RESPONSIBILITY?	WHAT IS THE SOURCE OF YOUR CRITERIA?
Example: Vacuuming rug	W	W	Woman's work	How I was raised
1. Disciplining children				
2. Grocery shopping				
3. Keeping checkbook, finances				
4. Preparing meals				
5. Ordering, when out to dinner				
6. Initiating sexual activities				
7. Driving the car				
8. Mowing the lawn				
9. Washing dishes				
10. Choosing furniture				
11. Choosing entertainment				
12. Choosing vacation spots				
13. Shopping for children's clothing				
14. Deciding method of birth control				
15. Feeding the children				
16. Doing the laundry				
17. Making the bed				
18. Granting children permissions				

Discuss the results with your partner before making a final expectation list.

as we were pedaling merrily along we approached a T intersection. Neither of us called out a preference in direction, and we collided. Even in such a simple matter as bike riding someone must take charge. Coleadership has gained popular acceptance today, but actually it is difficult, if not impossible, to accomplish, because a leader always emerges in a group situation.

The competition that results from the power struggle ends in bitter and resentful partners and confused children. Competition is known as one of the vicious enemies of a successful relationship. In marriage a couple desires intimacy, understanding, and reinforcement of self-worth, not competition.

A Supportive Relationship

I would like now to introduce an alternative role pattern, which I have termed "a supportive relationship." It is based on the Christian concept of mutual submission as a way of life in all interpersonal relationships. In a supportive relationship both partners willingly give up absolute power to dictate and control. Neither demands that his or her way is the only way and insists on unquestioned obedience. Rather, each shows a readiness to negotiate and adjust differences until common ground is established.

There will be occasions when the husband will lead because of his competence in certain areas. In other areas the wife will lead out because of her capabilities. Both parties, however, agree that the husband will assume the responsibility for overall family leadership in accordance with Scriptural suggestions as they understand them.

Yes, in a supportive relationship the husband does lead. His role, however, is not that of a dictator but as a president

of a well-run organization where every employee forms part of the team that makes the firm a success. Thus, the president works very closely with the vice-president, his wife.

We utilize the president, vice-president method in our home. Harry is definitely president of the Van Pelt Corporation, but as any well-trained executive, he checks out his plans and decisions with his vice-president. I, as vice-president, have certain areas of responsibility that I carry out on my own because of my capabilities and inclinations. Others I check out with him. We hold frequent meetings between us to discuss plans and objectives. He respects my opinions, abilities, and experience, and he wants my maximum input in family matters.

A Supportive Husband

God's original plan for the family was that husband and wife should live together in perfect harmony. Before sin entered, God was the Ultimate Leader in the home, and Adam and Eve both submitted to Him. Mutual submission was a natural way of life for them.

The context of the Genesis account of the first family has led many to conclude that God designated Adam as the family leader. But surely God would not appoint man to lead and then fail to give him the potential qualities necessary for leadership. Some men have more capabilities than others, but all men have some, and leadership qualities can also be learned and developed.

However, Eve's role as "a helper fit for him" (Genesis 2:18, RSV) was of no lesser importance than man's position. Shouldering different roles should never mean inequality. God created men and women to complement each other, and thus marriage is an interdependent, supportive relationship. Although male and female roles may differ, they are equal in importance and both are necessary to the well-being of a healthy society.

Understanding Submission

When a man takes the leadership role in a marriage, it is easy for him to forget that mutual submission—not domination—is the goal. The supportive husband will put himself in his wife's shoes and view their married life through her eyes, recognizing that her

desire for a happy home usually exceeds his. Yet she is more or less dependent upon him—his leadership, understanding, judgment, and cooperation—to accomplish her goals.

She longs for a well-run, smoothly operating home with a devoted, contented husband and smiling, well-mannered children. She wants necessary conveniences, good health, plus opportunities and freedom for herself. Yet to accomplish these goals she needs her husband's active support, concern, understanding, wisdom, and guidance.

If in the name of leadership he denies her this fulfillment, serious consequences may appear. Her individuality may become thwarted. She may feel like a nonperson and attempt to get back at her husband in many insidious ways. A continual suppression of those desires near and dear to her heart can kill her tender, loving feelings. If she feels totally dominated and suppressed, she may develop headaches, ulcers, sleeplessness, or one of many other emotional cover-ups. She needs freedom to operate in her sphere, to make changes as she sees necessary, and to enjoy the encouragement of a supportive mate.

A wise husband, therefore, understands his wife's position and will not make unreasonable demands on her, but instead will be sensitive to her position. He will exercise mutual submission, not always giving in to all her wishes, but always dealing fairly with her. He can consider her feelings in matters, sympathize with her position, and recognize her rights in each issue. A supportive relationship maintains respect, fairness, and kindness daily.

A man needs to understand that a woman feels secure when she is functioning under his leadership. God told Eve, "Your desire shall be for your husband" (Genesis 3:16, RSV). The Hebrew word for "desire" meant to run after or to violently crave something, which indicates the strongest possible yearning for it.

A woman wants and needs to respond to a husband whom she respects, and his leadership can demonstrate in a tangible way his love and concern for her. Respect for her husband grows as she observes his efforts to guide the family. And in addition to other things, the magnitude of her respect enhances or diminishes her ability for a continuing sexual response.

Supportive Leadership

Most women, regardless of how traditional or liberated they claim to be, enjoy looking up to a politely aggressive male who radiates masculinity, who is also sensitive to a woman's needs and can evoke a positive feeling in a woman. The truth is that not many men know how to give "soft" leadership. But the man who truly desires to please his wife may wish to consider some of the aspects of supportive leadership.

Leadership differs widely from authoritarianism. Authoritarianism represses individual freedom; a leader allows freedom of thought and actions. Authoritarianism is uncompromising; a leader is understanding. Authoritarianism is unyielding; a leader is adaptable. Authoritarianism assumes no willingness on the part of another toward cooperation and therefore dictates; a leader manages, motivates, inspires, and influences in order to obtain willing cooperation toward a mutual goal.

Love keeps the balance in a leadership role, and therefore it demeans no one, allows open and honest discussion (even dissenting opinions), and includes a sound system for making decisions, solving problems, and setting goals. When a husband takes seriously the command to love his wife (Ephesians 5:25), he will establish a partnership in which he will never command his wife to obey but will wisely offer soft leadership that allows her to follow. Such supportive leadership will bring harmony and happiness to both and have God's blessing.

A *Family policies.* The leader, responsible for the direction of the entire household, initiates action toward determining family policies and makes decisions regarding their progress toward such goals. Under his leadership, rules of conduct for the family are established, and he sees to it that they are implemented. Naturally the wise, supportive leader will ask for his partner's opinions so that the policies and goals result from the input of both.

Some men misinterpret this position and become dominating and dictatorial. Such authoritarianism prohibits free choice, individual growth, interchange of ideas, and freedom to

change. A supportive relationship, however, leaves no room for a dictator.

B *Division of tasks.* Any president who tries to operate the firm all by himself without delegating authority will find himself alone. Similarly, a careful division of responsibility is necessary in a well-organized home so that each person may function in his or her area to the fullest potential. The duties of each may follow traditional patterns—with the wife housecleaning, cooking, shopping, caring for children, sewing, and washing. The husband's duties might include cleaning the garage, caring for the yard, maintaining the car, and repairing the home. But if the wife excels in home repairs and he in cooking, nothing need prevent either party from breaking out of traditional roles. Flexibility is the key to a supportive relationship.

Harry can sense when I've had a particularly rough day, and rather than leaving me alone in the kitchen to carry out my role, he often sets about helping *without being asked.* (If I had to ask, it wouldn't mean nearly so much.) His masculinity is not threatened by assisting with women's work. Likewise when he is involved in a yard or building project, you might find me holding boards, handing tools, and giving encouragement even late into the night. We are each willing to lend support as needed.

Working together with household tasks provides some companionship, but extreme sharing in all areas is not necessary or even advantageous. In fact, studies show that couples who share the most household tasks have the most role disagreements. The best pattern to follow, then, is not complete sharing or complete separation, but a help-as-needed program.

C   *Decision-making.* In a supportive relationship the partners will consult one another on issues that concern the family and its future. It is disappointing for one partner to discover that a major decision has been made without his or her knowledge. The mutual decision-making process reinforces equality and self-respect.

A husband should take his wife into his confidence, ask for her opinions on family matters, and listen attentively as she presents her ideas. He needs her advice, not just to second all his motions, but as a counselor who possesses an intuitive grasp of situations that he may not see. Her knowledge of a problem may be limited, but her advice may be more reliable than his, due to her emotional reflection on issues. He should give her full opportunity to express herself, and as she speaks he should read between the lines by observing her nonverbal communication.

He should respect his wife's individuality and not suppose that she must agree with every idea he presents. A supportive relationship allows room for both parties to think for themselves and

to retain their own opinions, interests, and activities. There may be times when a decision must be deferred or not made at all because of differing opinions. It may also be possible that each partner might make his own decision and live in harmony with it rather than conform to the wishes of the other. Supportiveness never bends to dictatorship.

Although each party should be attentive and responsive in helping the other solve problems that must be faced, this is particularly true for the

Who Does What?

Some couples have found that a mutually agreed upon written job division has helped them work out a successful supportive relationship. They list all the jobs that need to be done and then consider who has the time, ability, and expertise to get them done. They also consider who is more concerned with each area and who enjoys the task the most.

The following chart will help you do just that. In the column on the left list all the important family responsibilities. To the right put the initials of the mate to which that responsibility applies.

Family Responsibilities	Time	Expertise	Concern	Enjoyment
1.				
2.				
3.				
4.				
5.				
6.				
7.				
8.				
9.				
10.				
11.				
12.				
13.				
14.				

husband. A woman needs to feel that her husband understands the home crises that she faces and that she can talk with him about her troubles without feeling rejected. Passive husbands who yield little support or sympathy decrease marital happiness. In short, when a husband responds positively, he fulfills his wife's need to be understood.

D *The family conference.* Family conferences help reduce frustrations and maintain harmony in the home. They should be neutral times during which problems and concerns are shared and evaluated. Successful family conferences follow certain guidelines.

1. They should be held faithfully every week during an unhurried time, when everyone is in a reasonably happy frame of mind. They should be informal occasions with as many family members present as possible.

2. Each family member should have a part in preparing the agenda or be allowed to introduce matters for dis-

cussion during the conference. The agenda should include such things as the scheduling of family activities and outings, permissions, problem areas. Every item on the list should be discussed, no matter how trivial it may seem at the time. Laughing about the small things and inviting cooperative efforts to solve major problems can promote family harmony. Personal problems should, of course, be discussed on a one-to-one basis.

3. End the family conference on a positive note. Encourage each family member with words of sincere appreciation for past performance as well as present efforts.

E *Personal decision-making.* Whether we like it or not, problems constitute part of life. Therefore, it is essential that each spouse knows how to make decisions in his or her area of responsibility. It is important in a supportive relationship to be able to gather information, analyze it, draw conclusions quickly, and come to a firm decision. The following suggestions may help you improve your decision-making process:

1. *Seek divine guidance.* People often work backward in their attempts to come to a decision. They may study, analyze, wrestle, and hassle a problem for days before finally submitting it to the Lord. Or sometimes they may bungle it entirely and then run to the Lord to bail them out. A preferred method is to approach Him first for guidance.

2. *Gather the facts.* Before you can make an intelligent decision, you must have knowledge about the situation. Once you have all the information together, you are ready to pursue possible alternatives. One of the best methods of

considering alternatives comes through "brainstorming." In brainstorming, husband and wife as a team, and even the children if the subject is suitable for them, explore every possible solution that pops into mind no matter how ridiculous it may sound. Every suggestion is considered as a possible solution. Comments such as "That's a dumb idea!" or "Grow up!" are not allowed, since they would shut down the expression of free thought. Try for as many suggestions as possible. When you feel you've gathered all the options, you're ready for the next stage.

3. *Weigh the information.* Many of the suggestions can be crossed off immediately. Others will need careful evaluation in light of your personal values, experience, discretion, understanding, and the experience of others.

4. *Make a decision.* The test of your decision-making ability is the capacity to choose the best alternative from the list of possibilities—like which dress to purchase, what brand of washing machine to buy, which job to accept. This process goes on unconsciously every time you make a decision. Without it you will misread the facts, misunderstand them, or fail to reach the proper conclusion.

The responsibility that goes with

Problem Areas

As husband and wife work toward a supportive relationship, implementing decisions and procedures will come easier. But stalemates will still arise. When they do, both must ease up a bit rather than try to force the other into obedience. Each should put himself or herself in the other's place and attempt to understand the resistance. Each should analyze his or her own attitudes. Why is he resisting me? Have I neglected her in some way? Have I failed to carry out any of my responsibilities? Have I shown poor attitudes in the past? Am I being unreasonable?

Adapting to a decision with which one does not agree is difficult. Sometimes a little patience is required for one to gather the forces necessary in order to keep from feeling like the little boy who said, "My daddy told me to sit down, but I'm standing up inside." Since force is the opposite of love, in a supportive relationship there will be no resorting to force or authoritarian methods. If cooperation fails to come, the husband might best rethink his plan. If this fails, too, it would not be beneath the dignity of a supportive husband to defer to his wife's wishes.

A husband may hate to admit it, but from time to time he will blunder in his attempts to guide the family through the maze of confused values in the world. Such failure may dampen his male ego at times, but he must learn not to judge his masculinity by worldly standards of success. At times he may even find it necessary to make things right with his wife and children. A real man can say that he is sorry, for there is no substitute for such straightforward honesty. Harry would say it like this: "Nancy, I blew it. I was stubborn and unreasonable last night. I'm sorry. Will you forgive me?"

decision-making can be awesome. A poor decision involving a family member can hamper one's relationship with that person. A financial mistake could mean that the entire family might have to suffer in order to help pay for it. But a poor decision is better than no decision at all.

And when a poor decision has been made, both partners must refrain from saying, "I told you so!" Instead, mistakes must be accepted, lived with, and learned from. Part of the dynamics of a supportive relationship involves growing through blunders.

Spiritual Leadership

Whether he realizes it or not, a husband has a more decisive influence upon his wife's spiritual health than anyone else on earth—his example and behavior influencing her for good or evil. A husband cannot hide his hypocrisy from his wife. If within the privacy of their home he treats her unlovingly or unjustly, nothing that he says or does in church can counterbalance such a demoralizing influence. A husband who loves his wife in a supportive relationship will be concerned not only about his own relationship to the Lord but also about her spirituality. He will not abdicate his responsibility by piously repeating, "That's between her and God. It's not my affair."

Although each one of us must ultimately stand before God alone and cannot slough off our lack of spirituality on someone else, the husband should take the initiative in conducting and scheduling daily family devotions. Too many men have pawned this responsibility off on their wives, and women have to bear more than their fair share of spiritual activity in the home.

Protective Leadership

A woman also needs the protection of her husband. She needs shelter from the rougher elements of life—not only from physical assaults but also from emotional and spiritual traumas. If an irate landlord bangs on the door and lets loose a multitude of complaints, she might reply, "I'll speak to my husband about it." She uses this not as an out but as a natural response from one living under the protection of her mate.

A supportive husband will protect his wife from any abuse that the children might mount against her. Should he hear the slightest word of disrespect or lack of obedience to her word, he should put a stop to it immediately and firmly. The mother should not have to battle for her children's respect. They should know that behind Mother's word lies Father's authority.

Larry had argued over something with his mother, and when she left the room he shouted after her, "You're a big dummy!"

Instantly his father's arm caught him by the shirt and lifted him right off the floor. "Who's a dummy?" Father demanded.

Larry blubbered, "I'm a dummy, I'm a dummy!"

His older brother burst out laughing, and his father could scarcely suppress a smile. His self-incrimination saved him from a spanking, but he never forgot the lesson that if he was disrespectful toward his mother, he would rile his father.

A husband's protectiveness over his wife also saves her from spiritual attacks. When a woman lives under the protection of her husband, she can move with great freedom in spiritual things as well as all other matters. God intended that the man stand between

A Quick Look

A majority of couples have never considered how they arrive at decisions, and yet this is vital to an understanding of a supportive relationship.

Respond to the following questions separately to see if the mutually supportive principle is functioning in your household.

1. a. Who makes most of the decisions in your relationship? b. How do you think your spouse answered this question?

2. a. Have you established guidelines to distinguish between major and minor decisions? If so, what are they? b. Who decided them?

3. What procedure do you generally follow when there is an impasse but a decision must be made?

4. How do you decide on assigning responsibilities for household chores?

5. a. In what areas of family living do you have the right to make decisions without consulting your mate? b. Who decided this policy, and how was the decision arrived at?

6. Do you find that you make the decisions you choose to make or more often do you make only the ones your mate does not want to make?

7. a. Do you have any "veto power" over your spouse's decisions? b. If so, what is the basis for it, and how was that decision arrived at?

8. a. How much do your children have to say about rules for their life in the family? b. Are they allowed to make any decisions without consulting you? c. How do you think they feel about the present arrangement? (Ask them. You might learn a lot.)

his wife and the assaults of the world to absorb many of the pressures that might strike her. However, a husband need not carry such protection too far. Some women have been so protected by their husbands that they have not only felt a loss of personhood, but when the husband died they floundered in total helplessness. Each needs to protect and support the other as individual crises arise. For example, the man who has tasted the buffering and soothing prowess from the depth of a woman's protective nature has tapped the counterpart to his own protectiveness. This again emphasizes the mutuality of a supportive relationship.

A Supportive Wife

My involvement in family life classes has opened numerous television opportunities for me. After a solo shot in Calgary one night, the moderator, cameramen, and group from the control room escorted me off the sound stage with a multitude of questions and comments. The most interesting one came from the host who had interviewed me. "Mrs. Van Pelt," he ventured, "you aren't at all like any of the popular books I've scanned on womanhood."

With a laugh, I asked him not to repeat that to any of my students, but I understood the meaning behind his words. He and the entire group had become genuinely intrigued by my presentation. They had not expected a woman to speak out on the subject of traditional marriage animatedly, humorously, and forcefully. They had envisioned the typical "submissive wife" as an opinionless doormat, an abject slave catering to every whim of her superior lord and master, and a whining martyr who works her fingers to the bone—in short, a woman with no personality, originality, individuality, or identity.

As I see it, God's plan for marital happiness includes supportive mates. Instead of competing for the leadership role or becoming a nonperson under total domination, a supportive wife not only allows her husband to lead but also encourages his leadership through her support of his decisions.

Even though she adapts her life to that of her husband's, she strives to be just as capable, intelligent, industrious, organized, efficient, warm, tender, and gracious as the ideal woman described in Proverbs 31. She is neither servile nor a household drudge, but she is the executive vice-president of the family firm. Marriage is a complementary, supportive relationship, and the key word is *supportive*.

The Meaning of Submission

Submission is not a dirty word, nor need we whisper it. When we recognize the Biblical goal of a supportive relationship, it becomes clear that submission doesn't imply that a woman is inferior to a man or that she must be totally subservient to him. And anyone who interprets such scriptures as Ephesians 5:22 and 1 Peter 3:1 in this way has it all wrong. These texts need not strike fear into the heart of the average Christian woman, because these verses do not make women out to be second-class citizens.

The Christian concept of mutual support means that submission in feminine terms implies that a wife willingly adapts her own rights to that of her husband—words that sound rather awesome only if viewed outside of a supportive relationship.

What Submission Is Not

"Do you think I am submissive to my husband?" I asked nearly two hundred young college women during a seminar on preparing for marriage. We all had a good chuckle over their negative responses. One said I was "too tall" to be submissive, and another said I "talked too much!" What crippled ideas we have concerning the meaning of submission.

Not many years ago I had to grapple with the question of submission to my husband, and it wasn't a joke. Could a strong-willed, dominant person such as

I am submit? In high school I had been leader, team captain, director, manager, and supervisor of nearly everything there was to lead, direct, manage, or supervise. Was this what I wanted for my marriage? Somehow I had to come to grips with the overall concept of what it means to be a submissive wife in a supportive relationship.

My study revealed that a doormat wife was just as far from God's ideal as is the henpecked husband. Neither extreme was ever intended for a compleat marriage. The Christian direction is for mutual submission, but at the point of conflict the wife is encouraged to submit, adapt, or yield. This, however, does not mean that a wife remains silent, leaving everything to the discretion of her husband. If she feels she has an insight or special understanding of a matter, she is obligated to share this with her husband so that he can take her opinions into his decision. If she withholds her feelings and knowledge on the matter, she is being less than submissive, for she has not given a willing response.

Submission does not mean helplessly depending on a man by refusing to accept responsibility or making decisions when necessary. A wife has her obligations and should remain free to carry them out. When decisions need to be made, she checks out her plans with her husband and assumes responsibility from that point on. If he is not available to consult, she acts in accordance with her best judgment.

Nor is submission servility. A wife who perceives her husband's judgment as wrong or disastrous to the family's welfare should tell him so—with respect, but firmly and honestly. If an issue arises and a wife says, "Do whatever you think is right, dear," and never offers an opinion even when she sees that her husband is heading for trouble, she is not submissive, but foolishly servile.

Blind obedience isn't the answer either. A woman who accepts an inferior position to her husband will lose his respect. Likely she has already lost respect for herself or will soon do so when she does not allow herself to be a real person. An intelligent husband does not want a doormat.

The extremes of silence, helpless dependency, servility, and blind obedience are not attributes found in a supportive wife. A supportive wife possesses dignity, opinions, and spunk, but she also respects and responds to her husband's supportive leadership.

What Submission Is

A submissive wife will willingly adapt her own rights to those of her husband, but how does this idea actually work in a supportive relationship? How far can a woman go in pushing her rights?

My husband expects to hear from me on major issues involving the family, and if I say nothing, he *knows* something is dreadfully wrong. If he makes a definite decision regarding the matter, I usually accept it. If for any reason I feel

that he hasn't considered all the angles, I will push it a little further. At this point he may change his viewpoint, but if he gives me a flat no, I do my best to accept it. Other times I might be so outspoken as to say, "You may think you are right from your point of view, but I'm right from mine!" We may never agree on his decision, but I feel better because I can express my opinions. This freedom of expression is part of a supportive relationship too.

The adaptiveness required in submission is actually an attitude before it becomes an act. It isn't a matter of the best atmosphere for creativity and individuality to express itself in a wholesome way. God wants us to fully express His gifts to us of intelligence, insight, and common sense. Everyone's personhood in a happy marriage must be preserved at all costs.

Another aspect of submission is respect. A husband's and wife's respect for one another sets an example to the children. Fathers and mothers strive to teach their children cheerful obedience, but their training will be effective only when children see their parents leading the way.

Sometimes one spouse or the other is totally unaware of how many times in how many ways he or she is breaking down respect for the other. The mother may say, "Dad is boss," but deep in her heart she knows this is not true, for she generally does as she pleases if there is a conflict of wills.

Children quickly notice when we fail to practice what we preach. If they see that Mother and Dad practice mutual respect, such an example cannot fail but to influence them. Every child needs a hero. A mother can help her children think of their father in this light rather than the Six Million Dollar Man. Her attitude toward her husband will count in the children's eyes.

"The noted criminal judge Samuel Liebowitz says, 'If mothers would understand that much of their importance lies in building up the father-image for the child, they would achieve the deep satisfaction of children who turn out well.' Perhaps, then, he suggests, she would not have to stand before him in juvenile court with tears in her eyes to say those words he hears so often: 'What did I do that was wrong, Judge—what did I do that was wrong?' On the basis of his long experience, the judge offers a nine-word principle for

mechanical obedience but a positive inner attitude. A wife might bend to every wish of her husband, but submission means *willingly* adapting to the rights of the other. So if it isn't done willingly, it isn't true submission. Underneath all her apparent compliance, she might be nursing insidious hurts and resentment that are stockpiling into a major case of bitterness. Sooner or later such rebellion will burst into the open and must be dealt with.

A submissive attitude will not stifle a woman's personality, or any personality for that matter. Instead, it provides reducing juvenile delinquency—'Put father back at the head of the family' '' (J. Allen Peterson, *The Marriage Affair*, p. 72).

Sometimes a woman may wish her husband would assume more leadership in the family, but she may be unconsciously failing to allow him to do it. She may be bucking his every idea or criticizing his faltering attempts to exert leadership. A woman can destroy her husband's efforts by saying, "I told you so," when he fails.

A supportive wife will encourage even feeble attempts at leadership by showing her appreciation. When her husband makes a suggestion, she can decide to accept it graciously even if she doesn't feel like it. Chances are she would have accepted the suggestion if someone other than her husband had made it. If a wife's attention and appreciation reinforce her husband's attempts at leadership, he will want to try again.

Difficult Situations

A husband who isn't worthy of respect. One of the first objections women raise regarding their failure to adapt to their husband's leadership is, "My husband isn't worthy of respect. He's mean, cantankerous, and ornery." However, we must differentiate between a person's position and his personality. It is possible to respect a person's position while recognizing personal deficiencies that need correction. All leaders have deficiencies of one kind or another, but God works through them. God will not hold a wife accountable for her husband's meanness, cantankerousness, or orneriness, but He

will hold her accountable for her *response* to him, for the way she chooses to react.

A husband with weak leadership skills. How can a wife adapt to someone who seems weak, who has failed previously, or who lacks leadership abilities? This is one of the hardest tests of submission—to step out of the way and let a man fail without interference. However, often men will begin to accept responsibility when their wives stop assuming it, when they are allowed to feel the full weight of leadership. Sometimes all a wife needs to do is let go and let her husband take over. Other times she needs to test her capacity to submit by allowing herself to go to the limits of submission. The ultimate goal in submission is not the attitude of, "How far must I go in submitting to this man?" but rather with delight, "How far can I go in adapting my needs to meet his without transgressing God's Word?"

A husband who isn't a Christian. Often a wife's spiritual awareness runs deeper than her husband's, and she may use this as a pious excuse for not adapting her rights to those of her husband's. She feels entitled to counter his wishes in matters of Christian education, church attendance, baptism, Bible study, discipline of the children, and many other matters. The Living Bible states: "Wives, fit in with your husbands' plans; for then if they refuse to listen when you talk to them about the Lord, they will be won by your respectful, pure behavior. Your godly lives will speak to them better than any words" (1 Peter 3:1*).

A continued attitude of respect and willingness to adapt, even when it goes contrary to a woman's thinking, will allow God to work matters out in a superior manner. Adapting will often

*The Living Bible, Paraphrased (Wheaton: Tyndale House, 1971). Used by permission.

How Do You Feel?

The following exercise has been designed to help you get in touch with your feelings regarding your relationship. Remember to distinguish carefully between "thoughts" about roles and "feelings," which are emotional. Complete the exercise and then share your responses with your mate. At points where negative feelings are expressed, negotiations should take place or else the relationship will remain static.

1. When my partner consults my opinions on family matters, I feel . . .

2. When my partner fails to consult my opinions on family matters, I feel . . .

3. When my partner dominates in family matters, I feel . . .

4. When my partner fails to show interest in family leadership, I feel . . .

5. When I treat my partner as an equal, I feel . . .

6. When I treat my partner as an inferior or as less important than myself in the relationship, I feel . . .

7. When my partner shows respect for my viewpoints, I feel . . .

8. When my partner fails to show respect for my viewpoints, I feel . . .

9. When my partner practices the principle of mutual submission, I feel . . .

10. When my partner fails to practice the principle of mutual submission, I feel . . .

11. When I practice the principle of mutual submission, I feel . . .

12. When I fail to practice the principle of mutual submission, I feel . . .

13. When I have dominated my partner, I feel . . .

14. An area of our role relationship that makes me feel good is . . .

15. An area in our role relationship that disturbs me is . . .

16. When my partner does not agree with my opinion, I feel . . .

soften her husband's contrary attitudes toward Christianity, for he cannot help but respect a faith that leads her to give so much of herself to him.

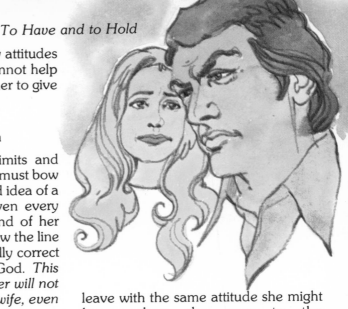

The Limits of Submission

Submissiveness has its limits and does not mean that a woman must bow stupidly to every evil wish and idea of a depraved man. God has given every wife a conscience and a mind of her own to use, and she must draw the line on what she believes is morally correct according to the Word of God. *This very subtle and delicate matter will not always be the same for each wife, even on identical questions.*

The mother must protect her children from moral, physical, and spiritual harm. Should the father give a child some form of drugs, physically abuse him, or mistreat him morally, the mother must step in. Even then she should make every effort not to break down respect between child and father. She might explain to the child that Daddy does not always do everything right as we see it and that we must be patient with his sins just as Jesus is patient with our sins. She must teach him by word and example to love and respect his daddy through it all.

When the wife is a Christian and the husband is not, he may want her to accompany him to amusements that she does not condone. What can she do in these cases? She should draw the line according to the principles found in Galatians 5:19-21. She has no obligation to obey him if he intends to lead her into evil practices, but she will leave all condemnation to the Holy Spirit. When she must say no, she can do it with love and respect, and attempt to make it up to him in other ways.

If she wants to go to church and he doesn't, she should go. But she should leave with the same attitude she might have when she goes to the supermarket—kiss him good-bye with no attempt to make him feel guilty for not attending with her. Neither should she "church" him to death with meetings several nights a week—leaving him home alone.

If he refuses to take charge of family devotions, then she will have to do it. Should an opportunity present itself to invite him to join, she might say: "Honey, let's go in and hear the children's prayers together," or "Would you like to read them their Bible story tonight? You read so well." If he doesn't want to, then she must carry on alone. She may ask one of the children to bless the food at the table. If Father tries to teach the children that there is no God, then Mother should later teach them that there is, explaining that Daddy says this because he doesn't know God.

A woman facing such difficult problems needs a private time with God in order to gain strength to face each day. A supportive relationship is difficult enough to attain when both partners work toward mutual goals. But when the husband opposes her Christianity, the wife has even a greater need to prayerfully maintain harmony in the home. She need not parade her devotions as evidence of her spirituality. Rather, her life should witness to that fact. A daily time to meditate and pray will provide the wisdom she needs in knowing how to make the best of the circumstances facing her.

The Benefits of a Supportive Relationship

The home that functions in a mutually supportive manner has fewer arguments and less fighting or contention, and a natural peace settles over the entire family. Power struggles vanish, and a closeness results that would not be possible any other way.

The husband will grow in masculinity and self-confidence as he practices the traits of supportive leadership, while the wife will notice an improvement in her attitudes toward herself and the home as she responds and adapts in a supportive manner. Together, backing each other up, their roles will enrich their relationship and make their marriage more fun and enjoyable.

The children will learn a natural respect for the organization of the home, the school, the church, and society as a whole by observing the model in their family. Society will also benefit. Our homes are the basic unit of society, and only when a home is functioning successfully, is a house in order. When a home is in order, the community, the church, and the nation can function as they should.

Further reading you will enjoy...

Andelin, Aubrey P.   *MAN OF STEEL AND VELVET*, chapters 2-9.
Beardsley, Lou.   *THE FULFILLED WOMAN*, chapters 2-12.
Benson, Dan.   *THE TOTAL MAN*, Chapter 12.
Cooper, Darien.   *YOU CAN BE THE WIFE OF A HAPPY HUSBAND*, chapters 6-8.
Dillow, Linda.   *CREATIVE COUNTERPART*, chapters 7 and 8.
Foster, Timothy.   *DARE TO LEAD*.
Hancock, Maxine.   *LOVE, HONOR, AND BE FREE*.
Kilgore, James.   *BEING A MAN IN A WOMAN'S WORLD*.
Mayhall, Jack.   *MARRIAGE TAKES MORE THAN LOVE*, chapters 24-29.
Stanley, Charles.   *IS THERE A MAN IN THE HOUSE?* chapters 24-29.

"Sex life in marriage is not automatic any more than it is only animal. It is an experimental, explorative adventure which two persons may undertake together over a long period of time. There are degrees of achievement in sex adjustment just as there are in all other aspects of marriage."
—W. Clark Ellzey.

Chapter at a Glance

Sexually Fulfill Your Mate

"I have never experienced a climax. This does not upset me, but my husband dwells on it constantly and therefore is never satisfied in sex. Can you help me?"

"How can I convince my wife that oral sex is OK? I want it, but she says it is a sin. What are Christian couples free to do?"

"I don't think sex should be a major part of life and certainly not receive top priority. Many scriptures indicate that sex is the biggest stumbling block for a religious person."

"All my husband thinks· about is sex! I don't mind it once in a while, but I do feel he carries matters too far. How much sex is too much?"

Healthy sexual satisfaction results from harmony in other areas of marriage. Only as a couple learn the meaning of genuine love, as they practice accepting one another at face value, as they work at the art of appreciating one another, as they learn the principles of effective communication, as they unravel individual differences and preferences, as they adapt to a workable supportive relationship of mutual respect and trust, can they expect a mutually

2. Vaginal
3. Multiple
C. Simultaneous orgasm
D. The afterglow
E. Religious women are—
   1. more sexually satisfied
   2. more sexually active
   3. most orgasmic

IV. Sexual Problems
A. Female orgasmic impairment
   1. Closely connected to feelings of self
   2. Barriers: bitterness, resentment, tired attitudes, fear
   3. Books, seminars, and tapes help
   4. PC muscle exercise
B. Premature ejaculation: controlling with the stop-start method
   1. Bring wife to orgasm
   2. Enjoy loving foreplay
   3. Entering and withdrawing
   4. Controlling the "point of no return"
   5. Extending intercourse
C. Male impotence

satisfying sexual experience. Allan Fromme refers to sexual intercourse as "body conversation," implying that both body and personality come in contact with each other during sexual union.

It takes time to adjust sexually after marriage. This sometimes comes as a shock to many couples who thought they would attain instant harmony. Research shows that most husbands and wives marry with little specific information concerning the physiology of sex or the emotional factors regarding the op-

posite sex. It takes time, understanding, patience, study, experimentation, and open discussion before a couple can master the ultimate in a fulfilling sexual relationship.

Frequency

A common problem in marriage arises when one mate desires sexual relations more frequently than the other. Although men most frequently make this complaint, more recently women, particularly in the over-forty age bracket, are also wishing for more frequent sexual intercourse. Statistics on frequency tend to make us preoccupied with numbers, but studies of committed Christians indicate that coitus three times a week is average during the entire course of marriage.

Frequency depends, however, on a number of factors such as age, health, social and business pressures, emotional condition, the ability to communicate about sex, and many other variables. Hence "averages" tend to be misleading. Each couple must find a frequency comfortable for their desire and life-style without worrying about numbers. Even then their individual level will vary from time to time, depending on circumstances.

While both sexes exhibit variations of desire, not only from person to person but from occasion to occasion, men hunger for sexual release more consistently than do women—and for a physiological reason. The prostate gland contains a small sac that acts as a reservoir for semen. As this sac fills, men feel the need for sexual relief due to the overabundance of semen in the seminal vesicles. When the reservoir is emptied, the pressure is relieved.

Dr. David Reuben writes, "Most men operate on a 48-hour cycle—that is, they need sex that often to keep them

148

Sexual Attitudes Inventory

We live in a sexually-saturated society, yet many couples know little about sexual subjects. The following questions are frank, and they deal with common problems that sexual counselors encounter. A great deal of hurt, frustration, and fear could be eliminated if such issues were dealt with before they became crisis situations in what God designed to be a beautiful experience.

Answer the questions below and then share your answers with your mate in free communication of feelings and thoughts:

1. How important is it for me to reach a climax during all sexual relations?
2. How do I feel about my partner's reaching a sexual climax?
3. What have I done in order to help my partner to reach a climax?
4. What feelings do I have about waiting for my partner to reach a climax?
5. I have cooperated in arousing my partner by . . .
6. When I don't have an orgasm, I feel . . .
7. When I do have an orgasm, I feel . . .
8. The sexual activity that arouses me most is . . .
9. When I talk to my partner about what arouses me, I feel . . .
10. When I initiate sexual activity and my mate turns me down, I feel . . .
11. Orgasm for me is the experience of . . .
12. When my partner fails to respond during sexual activity, I feel . . .
13. When I fail to respond during sexual activity, I feel . . .
14. When I see my partner nude, I feel . . .
15. When my partner sees me nude, I feel . . .
16. When my partner undresses me as part of foreplay I feel . . .
17. The frequency with which I find myself desiring sex is . . .
18. My mate's opinion of intercourse is . . .
19. My present attitudes toward intercourse are . . .
20. Hebrews 13:4 states: "Marriage should be honored by all, and the marriage bed kept pure" (NIV*). What does this say to you?
21. After reading 1 Corinthians 7:3-5, what concepts do you think the writer is trying to convey?
22. I have the following unresolved questions about sexual matters:
23. How honest were you about your true feeling (not thoughts) when you answered these questions?
24. How tense were you when you answered these questions?

---

*From The New International Version. Copyright © 1973, 1978 by the New York Bible Society International and is used by permission.

on an even keel." Another writer has reckoned that a healthy man's semen builds up every 42 to 78 hours and produces a pressure that needs release.

The male's desire for frequency sharply contrasts with the female's. Not only do men and women differ vastly in desire, but there are also enormous differences between women. Approximately 20 to 25 percent of all adult females might be termed "inhibited," which means that they express negative or lukewarm attitudes toward sex. Two percent are frigid or totally unresponsive in sex, and another 2 percent possess a high sex drive. However, 20 to 25 percent of all women demonstrate an excited attitude—that is they desire sex, seek it, and initiate it frequently. The remaining 40 to 50 percent register only average sexual interest.[1]

Among women, upswings in sexual desire may occur just before or just after menstruation or around ovulation. Sometimes sexual desire continues throughout menstruation, and apparently some normal women never feel voluptuous except during their periods. Both men and women need to be conscious of this cyclical change in a woman's sexual interests.

When the needs of one mate are greater than the other, happiness demands compromise. When a husband's needs are stronger than his wife's, he does not have to demand intercourse at his every whim, but she can go out of her way to meet his needs as an expression of her love for him. A sexually satisfied person is far easier to live with than one who isn't.

Let's Talk About It

Whenever a problem arises in a couple's love life, they tend to eliminate the topic from their conversation in hope that if they don't mention it, it will go away. For example, some couples *never* discuss their sex life. In a survey[2] I personally conducted of committed Christians, only 43 percent of the men and 38 percent of the women felt free to discuss sexual intimacies often with their mates. Ten percent of the males and 25 percent of the women never or only rarely did so. The most common reason listed by women for avoiding such discussion was that they felt embarrassed.

A survey by *Redbook* magazine in 1975 revealed a connection between good sexual communication and a good sex life. Of every 100 women in the study who stated that they always discussed intimate feelings with their husbands, 88 rated their sex life as very good or good. Of those who never discussed sexual feelings with their husbands, 70 in every 100 reported fair or poor sex lives. It appears that those who need to discuss their sexual problems the most, fail to do so, with resulting frustration and dissatisfaction marring their marriage.

Strongly religious women in the *Redbook* study were much more likely to discuss their sexual feelings than nonreligious wives. In fact, *Redbook* concluded, the data collected provide strong evidence that communication between religious women and their husbands is in every age group substantially above the average, while communication between nonreligious women and their husbands dips below average.[3]

Since women tend to feel more sexually inhibited than men and find it difficult to speak about sexual topics without embarrassment, whenever possible it is helpful for a husband to take the initiative in helping his wife verbalize her feelings. Both partners need to feel free to express honestly and frankly what feels good and what doesn't, what is desired and what isn't, what stimulates and what doesn't.

If a couple has never before verbalized their sexual thoughts and feelings, they should approach the topic slowly and carefully, and neither should become discouraged if the other reacts negatively. It takes time to discuss intimate feelings with ease. However, since all collective surveys indicate that the more open the communication on sexual preferences, the happier the sex life, the end results should be worth a try.

The Art of Foreplay

Foreplay, one of the most pleasurable portions of sexual expression, follows no set schedule on when to do what; therefore couples should understand one another's readiness for intercourse. The average woman reaches her maximum level of responsiveness after some twenty minutes of foreplay. In some cases an experienced wife may require only ten to fifteen minutes of preparation, an inexperienced bride as much as thirty minutes or even more, and a woman with a sexual problem forty-five minutes or more. A wife needs to understand that she is not abnormal

or frigid because she differs from the quick response of her husband. Because a woman responds more slowly than a man, she needs to be approached and wooed patiently, but she is just as capable of enjoying the sexual experience.

Women commonly complain that their husbands do not spend enough time preparing them. Some go so far as to say that they do not feel prepared at all. Women who are forced into sexual relations without the necessary preparations feel that their bodies have been exploited to gratify the needs of their husbands, without regard for their own needs. Such women often insist that they feel like prostitutes. Yet a little romantic tenderness throughout the day and a little more time at night would make all the difference in the world.

The wife of a husband who ejaculates rapidly and without sufficient foreplay usually will classify him as "ignorant" or "clumsy" in lovemaking. Yet the same husband often considers himself a good lover and reports that his wife achieves a climax to a higher degree than she herself reports. The truth is that fast lovers almost never make the most desired list.

A man, too, will benefit from lengthening foreplay. Not only will he sense a greater enjoyment from his wife's responsiveness, but he will also experience increased pleasure for himself. After the caress, erotic thought, or stimulating sight that brought on the erection, he enters a second phase of increased excitement that can stretch out to twenty minutes or more.

During foreplay a couple should engage in love play that both enjoy.

shaft

glans

scrotum

Usually the husband is the more willing to initiate a greater variety of lovemaking experiences, but he should not force these upon an unwilling partner. The key here is mutual enjoyment, and a couple can experiment with a great variety of pleasurable lovemaking experiences if they so choose.

Dr. Herbert Miles, a well-known Christian authority on sex, gives the following sound advice to couples in doubt: "In interpersonal relationships in the community and society, modesty is a queen among virtues, but in the privacy of the marriage bedroom, behind locked doors, and in the presence of pure married love, there is no such thing as modesty. A couple should feel free to do whatever they both enjoy which moves them into a full expression of their mutual love and in sexual experience.

"At this point it is well to give a word of caution. *All sex experiences should be those which both husband and wife want. Neither, at any time, should force the other to do anything that he does not want to do. Love does not force.*" [4]

Female Sexual Response

Male attention during lovemaking most often centers on the breasts and on the vagina, for both bring him much pleasure. However, although both are erogenous zones, the clitoris brings a woman her greatest sexual pleasure. It is located about one inch above the entrance to the vagina (see diagram on on page 154) and is comprised of a glans, a shaft, and a hood. When stimulated, it engorges with blood—much as the penis does—and throbs pleasurably.

According to the research of Masters and Johnson, the clitoris has no other function than to produce sexual pleasure. Termed "the trigger of female

desire," it is the most sensitive point for female sexual arousal. Yet it is not necessary for intercourse—only a vagina and penis are essential. Therefore, in a woman's anatomy God placed something additional in order that she might experience the same supreme sexual pleasure that her husband does.

Normally, during intercourse the penis does not touch the clitoris. Consequently most counselors recommend that the husband gently massage the clitoral area until his wife indicates that she is ready for entry. Dennis Guernsey likens the clitoris to the cornea of the eye: Just as one would never touch the eye directly, so the clitoris should never be touched directly. A better method is to massage the hood that covers it.

During this period of foreplay, a husband must not suspend stimulation of the clitoris, for a woman requires continuous stimulation to orgasm as opposed to the interrupted stimulation that serves adequately for most men. A man can, with practice, learn to insert the penis while continuing to massage the clitoral area.

Male Sexual Response

Sexual arousal for the husband begins with the erection of his penis, which follows within a few seconds of a stimulating sight, a caress, or amorous thought. From this initial stage of excitement, he progresses rapidly into the next phase if effective stimulation continues.

The penis, like the clitoris, consists of three parts: the glans, the shaft, and the base, and it is wrapped in a resilient, expandable sheet of skin (see diagram, facing page). The glans, located at the tip of the penis, is the most sensitive and responsive part of the male genitals and is the part he prefers to have stroked. Eighty to 90 percent of a man's sexuality centers in his penis and the nerve endings there.

He enjoys a gentle massaging of the genital region, also, for his second-most sensitive area is the scrotum, a saclike pocket of skin that hangs outside the body behind the penis. The woman must be careful not to apply excessive pressure to the testicles, however, since it causes a man as much pain as when he puts too much pressure on her clitoris. Most of her caressing should center around the top shaft of the penis. Stimulation here and fondling the head of the penis and the frenulum on the underside of the penile shaft will greatly increase his excitement.

Entry by Invitation

Prior to orgasm the husband places his penis into his wife's body. Even though she may have shown certain physical signs of readiness, such as vaginal lubrication, the husband should wait until her emotional response matches her physical response. Termed "entry by invitation," such an approach gives her control over when and how her body is to be entered. If someone

shaft of clitoris

hood of clitoris

glans of clitoris

vaginal opening

were to enter your home without an invitation, you would feel that he had invaded your privacy and would not be a welcome guest. So it is with a woman. When she is ready she can ask for entry.

The entrance of the penis into the vagina does not always signal for penile thrusting to orgasm. A pleasurable form of love play for the couple may be withdrawal and entering as many times as desired. In their mutual pleasure, they should focus not so much on sexual release as on the flexibility to enjoy the feelings of the moment and to have fun together. Sometimes their love play will be passionate and at other times more like fun and games. On still other occasions intercourse will primarily provide for sexual release, because those needs are more pressing for one or the other. Such a variety of purposes for intercourse are entirely acceptable and normal to marriage.

Orgasm

Orgasm for the male takes place in two phases. When the blood in his sexual organs has filled every available space, the muscles at the base of the penis contract, thus spurting about one-half teaspoon of seminal fluid out the end of the penis. Semen is primarily protein, similar to the white of an egg, and is neither dirty nor unsanitary, although it has a distinctive odor. Once the ejaculatory experience has been initiated by contractions, it cannot be stopped or delayed until the seminal fluid has been expelled. Although the woman can easily be distracted or interrupted in the midst of her orgasm, the man will carry out his two-phase experience—contraction and ejaculation—regardless of external stimuli.

Orgasm for the female is much more complex. Furthermore, confusion has resulted because of the vaginal-orgasm versus the clitoral-orgasm theory. A vaginal orgasm, according to the old school of thought, supposedly indicated emotional maturity and resulted from penile thrusting with no added stimulation of the clitoris. A clitoral orgasm supposedly resulted from manual manipulation of the clitoris. A woman who experienced the latter type of orgasm was regarded as psychologically flawed and immature.

To date no major study has ever proved a clitoral orgasm inferior to a vaginal. Indeed, it is now well documented that an orgasm is an orgasm. It is of no consequence whether it is a clitoral or vaginal response since the brain and the sex organs work together to produce orgasm. However, Dr. Herbert Miles has reported that only 40 percent of the women he surveyed attained vaginal orgasm without clitoral stimulation, and *The Hite Report*[5] found that only 30 percent of the 300,000 women studied could achieve orgasm regularly without clitoral stimulation. This means that for approximately 60 to 70 percent of the female population, penile thrusting does not lead to regular orgasm.

According to Tim LaHaye, the reluctance of loving partners to incorporate clitoral stimulation as a meaningful part of foreplay has cheated more women out of orgasmic fulfillment than any other single factor. Couples must not confuse manual stimulation of the clitoris with masturbation. Masturbation involves the manipulation of one's own genitals. It is basically selfish and excludes the happiness of the other person. Not so with clitoral stimulation during intercourse. God designed the clitoris to be used in sexual expression. It constitutes acceptable love play between husbands and wives, and for a majority of women it offers the only path to sexual fulfillment.

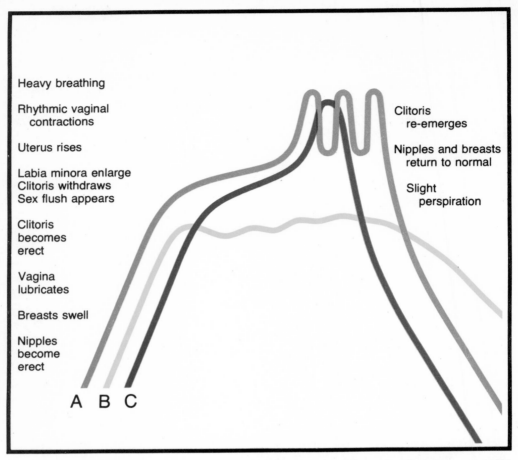

Heavy breathing

Rhythmic vaginal
   contractions

Uterus rises

Labia minora enlarge
Clitoris withdraws
Sex flush appears

Clitoris
becomes
erect

Vagina
lubricates

Breasts swell

Nipples
become
erect

Clitoris
re-emerges

Nipples and breasts
return to normal

Slight
perspiration

A B C

Three female climactic responses: (A) multiple orgasm, (B) orgasmic failure, and (C) single orgasm.

Multiple Orgasm

New research into female sexuality has shown that some women can experience many orgasms in a brief period of time (see diagram above). Men sometimes find this difficult to comprehend since they are powerless in most cases to regain their capacity without a rest of forty-five to sixty minutes. But a continuously stimulated woman is capable of five or more orgasms, often each one increasing in intensity. Most women in the Hite survey did not know this fact.

Because a woman can experience repeated climaxes, thoughtful men will often, after ejaculation, immediately stimulate the clitoral area so she can repeat the experience. It is the natural response of a loving husband to provide his wife with every pleasure. But multiple orgasms should not be forced upon a woman or expected during every sexual encounter. Most women prefer the experience on those special occasions when the circumstances, mood, and all the other factors work together. The single orgasm is still the most frequent response for a woman, and in the Hite

156

survey the majority of women reported a desire for only one orgasm.

Simultaneous Orgasm

The goal in intercourse is that both partners reach orgasm, but simultaneous orgasm is not necessary. The important factors are that both partners experience mutual pleasure, that both enjoy an orgasm, and that their love relationship is renewed. A procedure that works for most couples is for the wife to reach orgasm first, followed closely by her husband's. Each can then contribute to and share in the other's pleasure.

The Afterglow

Following sexual satisfaction the couple enters a phase of calm when body functions return to normal levels. At this point one of the main differences between male and female sexual response occurs. Men's bodies typically return to normal abruptly, and if a man follows his natural inclinations, he will probably turn over and fall asleep. A woman's body usually takes ten to fifteen minutes to subside. Because of this they often feel a strong need for their husbands to continue embracing them. Orgasm for women does not signal the end of lovemaking but merely an entry into another phase—the afterglow.

In my own survey, women shared their feelings with expressions such as: "I wish my husband wouldn't go to sleep so soon after intercourse." "I wish that he would hug and kiss me more after intercourse." "I wish he would still be as affectionate after his orgasm as before." "I like to feel him near me all during the night after intercourse."

Masters and Johnson, while researching sleep patterns following intercourse, noted that in the first hour after

sleep, wives usually moved nearer their husbands. When the husbands were removed from the bed, the women continued to reach for them and half the time settled in their places. Yet, when the wives were removed from the bed, the husbands stayed put and slept on. Following orgasm a woman seems to have a subconscious need to remain in touch with her husband.

Religion, Women, and Orgasm

A woman who considers herself a committed Christian has a higher chance of obtaining sexual satisfaction than a non-Christian. *Redbook*'s survey of 100,000 women shocked the world by announcing that "Religious Women Make Better Lovers"—that they are the most sexually satisfied, sexually active, and orgasmic women in the country.

Tim and Beverly LaHaye, authors of *The Act of Marriage,* [6] confirmed this information in a survey in which 81 percent of the women in their twenties experienced orgasm "most of the time," and another 11 percent "frequently." Thus, a total of 92 out of every 100 Christian women in their twenties experienced orgasm at least "frequently"—the highest figure reported to date in any survey. The same study also showed that 89 percent of the women in their thirties, 86 percent in their forties, and 84 percent in their fifties, achieved orgasm frequently.

The total percentage from my own survey checked out almost identically. Ninety-one percent of the women in all age groups experienced orgasm at least "sometimes." (Sixty-seven percent had an orgasm "all of the time," with 24 percent indicating at least "sometimes.")

Such information refutes the notion that religious women are too uptight to enjoy intercourse. On the contrary, it indicates that deeply committed Christian women feel freer and better about sex. They view sex as a gift from God, which leads to healthy attitudes regarding the importance of sex in marriage.

Female Orgasmic Impairment

Not many years ago the sexually unfulfilled wife was left to rot in her own sexual frustration. But that day is over, and modern research has proved that all married women are capable of orgasmic relief. Certainly no Christian wife should settle for less, for she owes it to both herself and to her husband.

A woman's orgasmic response is closely connected to her feelings about herself. Resentment, bitterness, misinformation, and tired attitudes erect sexual barriers for a woman that make it difficult, if not impossible, for her to respond to her husband. And since our most important sex organ is the brain, unless it says, "OK, go ahead," she cannot be sexually satisfied.

A woman who finds such attitudes blocking a satisfying sexual experience can help herself by adopting more positive attitudes. Such books as *The Act of Marriage* and *Thoroughly Married* may offer insight into her problems. Seminars and tapes dealing with sexual happiness are widely available. If such efforts fail to help, she should contact a trusted physician or ask for a referral if necessary.

Another method of increasing sexual pleasure for both men and women comes as a result of strengthening the pubococcygeus (PC) muscle. In 1940 Dr. Arnold H. Kegel, a specialist in female disorders, inadvertently discovered that an exercise to strengthen a weakened bladder muscle also increased sexual satisfaction for women. Not only did the Kegel exercise cure the patient's urinary problem, but also she experienced orgasm for the first time in fifteen years of marriage. Widespread reports now confirm Dr. Kegel's original discovery. The Kegel exercises have since been adopted by many physicians to improve the sexual response of patients, for perhaps as many as two thirds of all American women suffer from a PC muscle weakness severe enough to interfere with sexual functioning. An understanding of how the muscle works can relieve many cases of inadequacy.

The PC muscle runs between the legs from front to back like a sling. It supports the bladder neck, the lower part of the rectum, the birth canal, and the lower vagina. In two out of every three women, this wide muscle is weak and sags—thus interfering with sexual functioning (see diagrams on page 159).

The Kegel exercises to strengthen the PC consist of a series of contractions first utilized when urine is voided. If urination can be interrupted, the PC has been contracted. Once control of the muscle is learned, the exercise can be practiced anytime. Women should begin with five to ten contractions six times daily for the first week. Over a

(Left) Side view shows good pubococcygeus muscle tone. (Right) Side view shows poor pubococcygeus muscle tone.

six-week period, they should increase the number of contractions during the six daily sessions to fifty. Most women note changes in their sexual performance within three weeks of time, and after six to eight weeks a small amount of exercise will maintain the muscle tone.

Premature Ejaculation

While counseling a lady who had been a bride of just under a year regarding her sexual problems, I asked if her husband might be a premature ejaculator. "No, I don't think so," she responded. Then, on second thought, she asked, "What is a premature ejaculator?" I explained that the expression referred to a man who cannot control ejaculation for a period of time sufficient to satisfy his wife at least half of the time. I continued that this usually means the man ejaculates in two minutes or less after entry. At this point she nodded wonderingly and said, "Maybe he *is* a premature ejaculator."

Although premature ejaculation is essentially a male problem, it requires teamwork to rectify. The husband needs to admit his problem, and the wife must exhibit patient understand-

ing. At times she may become so frustrated that she may lash out at her "quick" husband, but such reactions will only heighten his feelings of inadequacy and complicate the situation. Furthermore, because premature ejaculation may have been a long-standing problem, no couple should expect an immediate solution. It can be resolved effectively and permanently, but the husband will have to learn new habit patterns, which takes time.

There are two main methods of treatment for premature ejaculation: (1) Masters and Johnson's "squeeze technique" and (2) the "stop-start" procedure. We shall explore the latter method here. It involves several steps.

1 *Bring the wife to orgasm first.* Since a premature ejaculator cannot concentrate on solving his problem while he is bringing his wife to orgasm, he should help her reach a climax first so that he can concentrate completely on his own sensations later. The husband can help his wife achieve orgasm by manual stimulation of the clitoris or another agreed-upon approach.

159

2 *Spend time in loving foreplay.* Recognizing that increased fondling heightens a man's excitement, a wife will often eliminate touching her husband's penis. In their effort to short-circuit excessive sexual tension, they proceed directly to intercourse. However, when penetration of that warm, familiar environment occurs without prior stimulation, a husband may actually thrust and ejaculate more quickly because of the total shock to his system. Therefore, the wife should lovingly fondle her husband's genitals—especially caressing the underside or head of the penis, but not to the point that he ejaculates.

3 *Entering and withdrawing.* During this state the husband inserts his penis (from the man-above position in which he maintains better control) *slowly* into the vagina—stopping penetration, or withdrawing whenever he feels the desire to ejaculate. (The friction of total withdrawal may trigger ejaculation, so it is preferable for the penis to remain in the vagina if possible.) Suspension of motion will not cause the erection to subside but will only curb the desire to ejaculate. When he feels in control, he can slowly begin entering or penetrating again. If the desire to ejaculate increases once more, he should stop movement or withdraw immediately. The objective during this phase is to penetrate until he senses imminent ejaculation. A man with a severe problem may not be able to insert more than the head of his penis before stopping to gain control.

4 *Controlling "the point of no return."* Sooner or later every man reaches "the point of no return" when he continues to thrust till ejaculation is completed. There is no turning back. During this part of the treatment, the man should approach the point of no return but maintain control by suspending motion. After deferring ejaculation, he then should rest from fifteen seconds to two minutes or more, depending on his problem—carefully timing himself by means of a clock with a sweep second hand. Although this sounds unromantic and clinical, it is important to do so until he can consistently recognize the sensation preceding ejaculation. During the time of suspension, he does not thrust, and she does not move, cough, sneeze, or wink, because the slightest movement could signal "the end" for him.

5 *Extending the act of intercourse.* Once the husband learns the feeling that occurs just prior to the point of no return, he can begin *light* thrusting motions. The objective is to tolerate gradually increasing amounts of momentum. At first he will have difficulty controlling his movements because his instincts and excitement motivate him toward deep thrusting. However, such deep thrusting does not usually produce the greatest amount of female satisfaction and can actually produce discomfort. Concentrating the motion closer to the vaginal opening is more advantageous for both husband and wife than deep penetration. It is better for her because only the first two or three inches of the vagina contain primary sensitive tissue, and it will reduce his excitement and thus assist him in learning ejaculatory control.

6

Lasting ejaculatory control. Once a man learns the sensations that precede ejaculation and can tolerate light thrusting with periods of rest, he is well on his way to ejaculatory control. After he can control ejaculation for fifteen seconds, he should increase the time to four fifteen-second periods. If he can learn to add one minute, he can eventually add two. And if he can add two minutes, he can add three. Soon he can engage in light thrusting, approach the point of no return, stop thrusting, and lose the desire for immediate ejaculation. After extensive practice, he will be able to maintain intercourse as long as he and his wife desire. A man attains complete ejaculatory control when he can select the time when his orgasm should occur.

The stop-start training sessions can produce increased pleasure for any couple. The husband can increase his

A Few Ideas for Her

Listed below are some creative ideas for spicing up your love life. Try several, and add a few of your own for variety.

1. Treat yourself to a new negligee rather than wearing the same old rag you have worn for years. Eventually build a wardrobe of nighties so that you have a variety of colors, lengths, and styles.
2. Give him a back rub, and end with gentle kisses at the neck area.
3. Allow him to undress you if he'd like to.
4. Purchase a low wattage colored bulb for a bedroom lamp.

Now add a few ideas of your own:

1. _____

2. _____

3. _____

Your project is to be loving and available this week. Prepare yourself mentally and physically for lovemaking. Then when the mood is right and you are ready, be the aggressor rather than the responder at least once. Now list one creative thing you will do in the area of your sexual relationship within the next month.

My creative project will be _____

Memorize one of the following texts: 1 Corinthians 7:4; Proverbs 5:18, 19; Song of Solomon 5:6. My verse for this week is

_____ .

ability to delay ejaculation and thus prolong the pleasures of intercourse, and the wife may begin to experience sexual arousal unknown to her before. If she has not had climaxes, she may now do so. If she has already reached this plateau, she may go on to enjoy multiple orgasms. Many couples also find that it frees them to experiment with various positions—an option never open to them previously, due to the shortness of time. Through teamwork they will have developed valuable verbal and nonverbal communication skills as well as a new awareness of their interdependence in bringing one another sexual fulfillment.

Male Impotence

Impotence affects about 10 percent of the total male population and results from a combination of circumstances. Emotional attitudes, such as anger, fear, resentment, and guilt, are causative factors. Ego problems, such as fear of rejection, can be devastating enough to negate normal functioning. Certain stress factors, such as obesity, poor physical fitness, heavy smoking and drinking, and depression, can contribute to impotence. A nonstimulating, passive wife can lead to boredom and impotence.

The methods for curing impotence are not as clear-cut as with frigidity in women with a weak PC muscle, but a man who honestly and frankly faces the problem has the potential for a complete recovery. Emotional factors dealing with anger, fear, resentment, and guilt can best be resolved by asking God for relief from them. The most difficult problem to handle might be ego problems that threaten masculinity. In these instances professional counseling might be advisable. A health and fitness reconditioning program can alter the stress factors involved.

The biggest hurdle might be mental attitudes toward the problem. The more a man thinks he is sexually finished, the more real the possibility becomes. When a man first encounters impotence, he should have a complete physical examination. If there is no physical malady, he can thus adjust his attitudes in a more positive manner toward success. A wife can help her husband during this time by sexual aggressiveness.

What Women Want and Need

A woman responds to a man in direct proportion to his ability to fulfill her emotional needs. By failing to create an atmosphere in which his wife can respond, a man can deprive himself of the sexual pleasure that is important to his happiness. He may wonder how she can say that she still loves him and yet deny him what he wants and needs most. But when things are out of balance in the sexual department, the husband might well look to himself, for there are not so many lukewarm or frigid wives as there are husbands who fail to meet their needs.

Lovemaking is a deeply emotional experience for a woman. She is stimulated by the amount of romantic love her husband has shown for her throughout the day and considers each lovemaking encounter a moment of profound love and a deep part of her life. If her husband seems to take their sex life for granted, she can feel deeply hurt and offended. Repeated assurances may seem unnecessary and theatrical to him, but not so to her. She does not need reassurance because she is vain or seeking flattery, but rather a woman withdraws instinctively from sexual encounters devoid of love and adoration.

A Few Ideas for Him

Here are some creative ideas for making your sexual relationship more interesting. Try several, and add a few of your own creation for variety.

1. Shop for a new wrap-around garment to wear instead of the same old white shorts she's seen you in for years. Bathe yourself and add a dash of her favorite cologne. Remember to brush your teeth, comb your hair, and shave (yes, again!).
2. Try a bouquet of flowers with a lighted candle next to it on the dresser.
3. Some soft romantic music might lend to the atmosphere.
4. Treat her to a telephone love affair. Call her in the afternoon and whisper a multitude of sweet nothings in her ear.

Now add a few ideas of your own:

1. _____

2. _____

3. _____

The only courting many men do begins and ends in the bedroom. Sex under these circumstances becomes a one-room affair. Why not plan a special date on a special day that ends in a special place? A long weekend away maybe. Or an overnight stay in a motel. Somewhere different. There is something exciting and romantic about planning a special time away together.

A woman has a special need to feel respected as a person, and unless she feels her husband's constant approval of her as an individual, she will be unable to enjoy making love. Since her self-esteem is closely related to her sexual enjoyment, she will seek reassurance in areas where she feels the weakest.

One's sexual nature is forever hooked up with the psychological nature. So if she feels ugly, she will be unable to respond without embarrassment. A shy person with deep-seated feelings of inferiority will express the same symptoms in the sexual life. Conversely, the self-confident, emotionally healthy individual is much more likely to have a well-adjusted sex life. Thus every husband should recognize that anything which reduces his wife's self-esteem will affect her performance in the bedroom. If he ever teases her— *even in fun*—about small breasts, skinny legs, or being overweight, she will become extremely self-conscious during sexual encounters.

Also, a woman does not have to

achieve an orgasm *every* time in order to enjoy sex. Many women can participate in sexual relations, not achieve orgasm, and yet feel fully satisfied, even though they enjoyed no ecstatic climax. Never should a husband *demand* that his wife achieve an orgasm, for such a demand would put her in an unresolvable bind. She might lose interest in sex altogether, or she might begin to fake orgasm. But most men despise the farce, and as Dr. Dobson points out, "Once a woman begins to bluff in bed, there is no place to stop. Forever after she must make her husband think she's on a prolonged pleasure trip when in fact her car is still in the garage."

Then, too, what turns men on is not what turns women on. A glimpse of her in a breezy nightie may be all it takes to flip his switch, and his thoughts race with excitement as he imagines what lies ahead. But she is wired differently. Although she may admire his masculine build and enjoy seeing him dressed in a racy sports outfit, this will rarely sexually arouse her. Similarly, the passionate kiss arouses him far more than it does her.

A woman needs to hear words and to experience feelings before she can respond in the bedroom. This subject got the most attention from the women in my sex survey. When asked what one change she would like to make in her mate's lovemaking ability, one woman replied, "Have him realize that the lovemaking atmosphere starts when he jumps out of bed in the morning—not when he jumps in at night. Little attentions, kind words, concern for me, touching, set the mood for me." Any husband who thinks he can merely walk into the bedroom and expect his wife to "turn on" with no preparation doesn't understand female sexuality.

Some men might also pay more attention to cleanliness and body care.

Perspiration, an unshaven face, halitosis, and general tackiness might well make some wives groan silently all the way to the bedroom. It is just as important that a husband be physically appealing for his wife as it is for her to be so for him.

A man who insists on a brief nighttime romp regardless of his wife's mood or her state of health will always end up disappointed in the quality of their sex lives. A highly sexed, egocentric, selfish man may experience maximum relief but minimum fulfillment, since he has never learned the meaning of genuine love. His enjoyment of sex will rarely rise above the frustration level.

Contrary to popular belief, women want more imagination and variety in sex, too. In my sex survey one young woman wrote, "My husband always does the same thing—number one, number two, and always says the same 'I love you' ten million times." Others asked for "a few more unusual overtures, more challenges." Any husband whose advances are always on the same night, at the same time, in the same place and position, has no imagination. The man who wants the wife of his youth to respond for a lifetime needs to create variety.

Men are the pursuers to a great extent, and women the responders. But women must have something to respond to. Even an inhibited woman can be responsive if her husband woos her gently, slowly, patiently, and creatively. What could be more exciting or challenging for a man than improving his sex life? Any man can become a better lover or even a great one if he works at it.

What Men Want and Need

A *Ladies' Home Journal* survey[7] of more than four thousand men listed an

164

The Intimate Hours Program

The intimate hours program was developed by Dr. Robert F. Kaufmann, a minister and marriage counselor, to help enlighten couples about their likes and dislikes in their sexual experience without threatening their relationship. Husbands and wives can discover not only the extent of the mate's preferences but also can make exciting discoveries about themselves.

Both husband and wife should sit down together and complete the questions. There are no right and wrong answers to the questions—no high or low scores. You may write out the answers or discuss your responses verbally—whichever is easier for you. It is important to complete the entire questionnaire at one sitting rather than dividing it into segments. Don't stop for lengthy discussions regarding a single item the first time around. Mark those questions and come back to them at a later time. You need not be limited by the answers listed. Add any answers you wish.

Make certain that no one else sees the answers to the questions but the husband and wife involved. Be completely alone with your mate without interruption so you can focus on each other. And give yourselves plenty of time.

1. Does your mate enjoy making love as much as you do? (a) always; (b) often; (c) sometimes; (d) rarely; (e) never

2. Does your mate want to make love as often as you do? (a) yes; (b) no; (c) don't know

3. The most satisfactory lovemaking occurs when—(a) you and your mate reach orgasm simultaneously; (b) the woman reaches a climax first; (c) the man reaches a climax first; (d) the woman has an orgasm, but the man does not; (e) the man reaches a climax, but the woman does not

4. Do you prefer making love—(a) in bright light? (b) in soft light? (c) in shadowy light? (d) in total darkness? (e) regardless of the lighting conditions?

5. If you have a TV set in your bedroom, do you—(a) turn it off before beginning any sex play? (b) turn it off after beginning sexual activity? (c) leave it on during sexual activity?

6. Something in sex intrigues you or your mate, but you have never engaged in it. (a) true; (b) false; (c) there was, but no longer; (d) don't know

7. If you make a purely affectionate move toward your mate, does that quickly arouse his/her desire for sexual intercourse? (a) too often; (b) often; (c) sometimes; (d) rarely; (e) never

8. How much time do you spend with your mate in foreplay? (a) too much time; (b) not enough time; (c) enough time

9. I would prefer that the entire sex act with my mate took (on the average)—(a) less time than it does now; (b) about the same time it does now; (c) more time than it does now

10. It is more important for you/your mate to—(a) have one or more orgasms during sex; (b) be assured that you/your mate is loved during sex; (c) be assured that you/your mate is loved after sex; (d) be caressed and fondled after sex

11. Presuming that your mate has an orgasm before you, is he/she still interested in activities that stimulate you to orgasm? (a) always; (b) often; (c) sometimes; (d) rarely; (e) never

12. Due to her mate's inattention to her after he has had an orgasm, a woman can sometimes feel used after sex. Have you ever experienced this in your relationship? (a) always; (b) often; (c) sometimes; (d) rarely; (e) never

Adapted from "The Intimate Hours," *Ladies' Home Journal*, June, 1978, pp. 48-52, which was adapted from *Better Sex, Better Marriage*, William Morrow and Company, Inc. Copyright © 1978 by Robert F. Kaufmann, PhD. Used by permission.

13. When you do something that pleases your mate sexually, does he/she indicate his/her pleasure? (a) verbally; (b) nonverbally; (c) not at all

14. Once a person has been aroused sexually he/she—(a) always wants or needs an orgasm; (b) sometimes wants or needs an orgasm; (c) never needs an orgasm; (d) probably enjoys sex with or without an orgasm

15. I prefer making love—(a) in the morning; (b) in the afternoon; (c) in the evening; (d) at night after dinner; (e) time does not matter

16. I find my mate sexier when he/she goes to bed—(a) completely covered by gown or pajamas; (b) wearing tops only; (c) wearing bottoms only; (d) no difference

17. Does your mate like to see you naked? (a) always; (b) often; (c) sometimes; (d) rarely; (e) never

18. I prefer sex most—(a) in my own home; (b) in a hotel or motel; (c) in a resort; (d) in a romantic place

19. I think my mate is sexually—(a) too aggressive; (b) aggressive enough; (c) passive; (d) too passive

20. During intercourse my mate and I generally use—(a) only one favorite position; (b) only a couple of positions; (c) several positions; (d) many different positions

21. I know just how to arouse my mate sexually, and I can do so (a) always; (b) often; (c) sometimes; (d) rarely

22. What are your mate's three most erogenous zones—those areas of his/her body where contact is most likely to arouse him/her? (a)   ; (b)   ; (c)

23. Are your mate's erogenous zones the same as they were when you were first married? (a) all of them; (b) most of them; (c) some of them; (d) one of them; (e) none of them; (f) don't know

24. What kind of sights, sounds, or aromas stimulate your sexual desires? (a) romantic stories; (b) certain kinds of music; (c) love stories on TV or film; (d) incense; (e) none of the above; (f) other

25. Which of the items listed previously diminish your sexual desires?
(a)   ; (b)   ;
(c)   ; (d)   ;
(e)   ; (f)

26. After an unpleasant discussion or argument with your mate, you should never go to bed angry and should have sex as a way of making up. (a) always; (b) often; (c) sometimes; (d) rarely; (e) never

27. Deviations from or experimenting with any methods of sex other than coital intercourse are—(a) perverted; (b) dirty; (c) interesting; (d) stimulating; (e) essential to marital sexual enjoyment

28. If the telephone rings while I am engaged in sex with my mate—(a) I ignore it; (b) I answer it; (c) if it is for me I answer it briefly and hang up; (d) if it is for my mate, he/she answers it briefly and hangs up; (e) my mate answers it for whatever length that conversation would normally take

29. It is more important that the wife keep her figure to remain sexually appealing to the husband than it is for the husband to maintain his physique in order to remain sexually appealing to her. (a) definitely; (b) probably; (c) possibly; (d) definitely not

30. If you found sex with your mate unsatisfactory for a considerable time, would or should you—(a) give your mate some sex books to read as a hint? (b) suggest changes? (c) become more assertive? (d) put up with unsatisfactory sex? (e) avoid sex on various pretexts whenever you could? (f) compensate by masturbating? (g) find more satisfactory sex elsewhere? (h) tell your mate directly and openly that his/her sexual performance bothers you?

31. When your mate wants to make love, he/she generally approaches you—(a) romantically; (b) seductively; (c) pleasantly; (d) in a matter-of-fact manner; (e) in the same way every time; (f) demandingly, as if it were your duty to have sex whenever he/she wishes; (g) saying or doing nothing other than hoping you want sex at the same time he/she does

32. When I want to show appreciation or love for my mate I attempt a supersexual performance—(a) always; (b) often; (c) sometimes; (d) rarely; (e) never

33. Do you withhold sex to get even for some real or imagined wrong? (a) always; (b) often; (c) sometimes; (d) rarely; (e) never

34. Does your mate withhold sex to get even for some real or imaginary wrong? (a) always; (b) often; (c) sometimes; (d) rarely; (e) never

35. How do you avoid your mate's sexual advances when you are not in the mood? (a) claim headache or other physical illness; (b) distract him/her with another conversation; (c) go out; (d) go to sleep; (e) complain about money; (f) show anger; (g) bring up children's problems; (h) watch TV; (i) read; (j) other

36. Arguments between you and your mate are generally resolved—(a) very quickly; (b) in fairly short time; (c) slowly; (d) only after a very long time; (e) frequently they are not resolved—just shelved

37. When you got married did you expect there would be periods of time—cycles—when your sexual activity with your mate would be substantially better than at other times and, obviously, times when it would be much worse? (a) yes; (b) yes, but I didn't anticipate either the extremes or the duration of the cycles; (C) no

38. Are you as conscientious now about your personal grooming habits when you go to bed with your mate as you were when you first went together? (a) always; (b) often; (c) sometimes; (d) rarely; (e) never

39. My mate tends to regard sex (a) very seriously; (b) too seriously; (c) with a little humor; (d) with a great deal of humor; (e) too lightly

40. Do you think that your sexual fantasies should remain secret and totally private? (a) always; (b) some of them; (c) no, they should be shared

41. Sexual fantasies—(a) enhance my enjoyment of sex; (b) diminish my enjoyment of sex; (c) destroy my enjoyment of sex; (d) have no effect on my enjoyment of sex

42. Is there something in sex that your mate once attempted with you that you did not like, rejected, or discouraged but that you would now like to try? (a) quite a few things; (b) a couple of things; (c) one thing; (d) nothing

43. Is one of you the dominant partner in lovemaking and one the submissive? (a) always; (b) usually; (c) no

44. Would you like to reverse these roles on occasion? (a) yes; (b) no; (c) sometimes

45. Do you prefer that sex with your mate—(a) be planned for a particular time—almost like a date? (b) be totally spontaneous?

46. Do you look forward to planning a time for lovemaking? (a) regularly; (b) sometimes; (c) no, I prefer spontaneous and unplanned sex

47. Do you tell your mate that you enjoy sex with him/her? (a) frequently; (b) occasionally; (c) rarely; (d) never.

48. Do you and your mate say, "I love you" with what you consider sufficient frequency? (a) yes; (b) no

49. Closely following orgasm, does your mate prefer to—(a) hold you? (b) talk? (c) turn on TV? (d) go to sleep? (e) other?

50. Following orgasm, would you prefer that your mate—(a) hold you? (b) talk? (c) turn on the TV? (d) go to sleep? (e) other?

unresponsive woman as the biggest turnoff and a cold, uninterested woman as what irritates men most during sex. Experts have concluded that during the initial phases of foreplay, a woman responds automatically to effective stimulation. But she must *learn* how to move toward and actively *seek* orgasmic release.[8] She cannot achieve it through passivity, regardless of how skillful her husband's techniques may be. She must surrender, not only to her own husband, but to her drive toward the release of sexual tension.

Few husbands will complain about a passionate, creative wife who responds with enthusiasm to his advances. One of the major sources of male dissatisfaction in my sex survey was a lack of aggressiveness and response from women: "I want my wife to be more aggressive and expressive. . . ." ". . . initiate sex and talk about it in terms of how to improve it. . . ." "for her to be the aggressor. . . ." ". . . that she would do more initiating—think more about it." And this latter husband promised, "I would work less and be less concerned about work."

The only portion of the sexual experience enjoyed by a man more than ejaculation is the satisfaction he derives from an amorous wife who finds him sexually stimulating. Sometimes, however, a Christian wife does not see creativity and responsiveness as part of a religious woman's demeanor. These women might be surprised to learn that 65 percent of their husbands wanted more interest, response, and creativity from their wives. Only 35 percent felt satisfied with the status quo.

Whereas a woman is stimulated primarily by experiencing the emotions of love, a man is stimulated to a greater degree and more quickly by sight. Men love to look at the female body, and they turn on at the glimpse of a nude or partially nude female. Yet one woman imagined her husband to be a "dirty old man" simply because he became aroused when she undressed before him at night. This frustrated both of them until she learned that his ready attitude did not constitute depravity on his part. Instead, he reacted this way because God designed his body to do so.

Although it isn't necessary to cavort in baby-doll pajamas and high-heeled boots a-la-Total-Woman style, Marabel Morgan's point is well taken in the face of stained bathrobes, flannel pajamas, and ragbag nighties. One of the assignments I give women during the lesson on sexual fulfillment is to purchase a new wardrobe of attractive nighties in all lengths and colors. (No husband has ever complained about this expenditure!) Not long ago, after I mentioned this assignment to a gentleman, he delightedly exclaimed, "And tell them *never* to wear pajamas!"

Sometimes women are troubled by Matthew 5:28, which reads, "Whosoever looketh on a woman to lust after her hath committed adultery with her already in his heart." This text means that looking becomes a sin only if it is translated into lust. A man's viewing of another woman's body won't tempt him to go to bed with her if everything is right at home. The first seeds of dissatisfaction usually begin with anger, bitterness, and resentment rather than with lust.

A man may use sexual contact in a variety of ways. Many feelings may come into play for him besides love and affection. He may have experienced frustration and discouragement due to a difficult workday and seek sex as an outlet. His desire may spring from sadness and loss in another area of his life. Or it could also result from a sense of pleasure that he received by some accomplishment. Few if any of these experiences have any direct connection with his wife, yet he seeks a sexual experience with her due to feelings generated by another sector of his world. Sex comforts a man. He seeks sex to satisfy other emotions in addition to love.

One of the main hindrances to a woman's interest in sex is fatigue. After she has struggled through an eighteen-hour day, sex can be the last item on her mind—and whatever gets done last probably gets done poorly. A loving wife will sort out priorities so that sex doesn't languish in last place. When 9:00 PM comes around, she will fight the urge to begin one final project before bed. The wife who considers the sexual aspect of her marriage to be important will reserve time and energy for it.

Men have been asked to lead out in initiating creativity during lovemaking, but women must respond to such efforts, or they will be in vain. Women, too, can be creative. A new look in the bedroom might be appreciated—new drapes, different lighting, or a rearrangement of furniture. An intimate candlelight dinner for two or a new

place and a new time for making love might be part of an occasional plan.

Married Lovers

Husbands and wives should aim to be imaginative, creative, and willing lovers. God designed that sex—unhampered by selfishness—be exciting, enjoyable, and fulfilling. Good sex, then, comes as the end result of a satisfying relationship. If you have sexual problems, do not look for the answers in your sex life itself but in the quality of your total relationship.

Further reading you will enjoy...

Beardsley, Lou. *THE FULFILLED WOMAN*, chapters 13-16.
Deatrick, Mary. *SEXUAL MATURITY FOR WOMEN.*
Deutsch, Ronald. *THE KEY TO FEMININE RESPONSE IN MARRIAGE.*
Dobson, James. *WHAT WIVES WISH THEIR HUSBANDS KNEW ABOUT WOMEN.*
Guernsey, Dennis. *THOROUGHLY MARRIED.*
LaHaye, Tim and Beverly. *THE ACT OF MARRIAGE.*
Landorf, Joyce. *TOUGH AND TENDER*, Chapter 7.

Health is: "a state of complete physical, mental, and social well-being and not merely the absence of disease or infirmity." —World Health Organization.

Balanced Living With Your Mate

T Adams

A curious four-year-old pressed his nose tightly to the glass display case in a candy store. His mother was in a rush and spoke impatiently to him: "Danny, hurry up and make up your mind. Spend your money and get it over with!"

"But, Mamma," he replied, "I have only one penny to spend."

Danny had only one penny to spend just as you and I have only one life to live, and we should consider carefully how we intend to spend it. Most people feel that they have the right to live just as they please. But God didn't design life that way. All life is regulated by a set of rules built in by the Master Designer.

When Adam and Eve came from the hand of our Creator, they were perfect—physically, mentally, socially, and spiritually in harmony with the laws of God. But sin disrupted this harmony, and our physical bodies have suffered the penalty—disease and death. Our mental faculties have also suffered, for our minds have become filled with evil. Our social relationships have deteriorated until divorce, crime, and hate seem to rule. Adam and Eve's natural desire

Chapter at a Glance

I. **All Life Is Regulated by Rules**
   A. Adam and Eve were created—
      1. perfect physically
      2. perfect mentally
      3. perfect socially
      4. perfect spiritually
   B. Sin has disrupted the harmony of Eden

II. **There Is a Way to a More Abundant Life**
   A. An ideal marriage is neared only when we develop to the utmost the—
      1. body
      2. emotions
      3. mind
      4. spirit
   B. Every aspect of our nature reacts upon the others
      1. The mind affects the body
      2. The body affects the mind
      3. Social problems lead to mental anguish
      4. Spirituality is a vital component of balanced living

Dealing With Family Crises

A family crisis can be either a catastrophe or an opportunity. It all depends on how you respond to it. Some people have learned constructive ways of profiting from every experience that comes into their lives. Others are thrown off-balance by even the slightest difficulty.

Evaluate your pattern of dealing with family crises by listing in the left-hand column some of the crises you have encountered. In the space to the right briefly describe how you handled each crisis.

CRISIS   HOW HANDLED

_____   _____

_____   _____

_____   _____

_____   _____

_____   _____

Often when faced with a crisis we say, "I just don't know what to do." But God has a positive way of dealing with every crisis if we will commit ourselves to constructive action and trust Him to bring the insight needed to resolve it. Remember this threefold axiom:

A—Affirm God has a plan

C—Commit yourself to constructive action

T—Trust God for insight into a solution

What examples of the ACT axiom do you find on your list?

_____   _____

First Thessalonians 5:18 says: "In every thing give thanks," and this means even when you encounter troubles. Family crises can become opportunities for growth. Using crises as opportunities for growth begins with a thankful spirit. If you have a thankful attitude, you are ready to experience the joy of trouble. Begin to develop a thankful attitude for trouble by writing a prayer of thanks. Go over your list of crises and evaluate what ways you can thank God for such difficulties.

to serve the Creator is gone. Self-serving supplants God-serving, and thus our spiritual nature has changed as well.

But there is a commonsense route back to a better, happier, fuller, more abundant life, and it's available right now if you'll fully use your physical, mental, social, and spiritual capabilities. Since we have a four-part being—body, emotions, mind, and spirit—the only way to approach a satisfying marriage is to develop oneself to the utmost potential in each of these areas.

An ancient parable illustrates the point of how important each part is to the whole being. About five hundred years before Christ's time, the people of Rome rioted against the governing nobility. They cried, "You great men have the titles—all we have is the toiling. You nobles have all the honors and wealth and security, but we common people suffer the consequences; we're paying the bill by our blood, sweat, and tears. We're sick and tired of being slaves to Rome's rulers!"

So, crowding the street, the mob moved toward a strategic part of the city, bringing the capital to such a state that the senators and great men of Rome fled for their lives. However, a famous hero of the people, General Menenius Agrippa, was sent among the crowd to quiet them, and he captured the attention of the rioters with a parable that Livy, the Roman historian, preserved for us.

"The various parts of the body planned a conspiracy against the stomach. They agreed that the hands would not place any food in the mouth. The mouth would not take any food offered to it, and the teeth would refuse to chew any food that went into the mouth. Thus they plotted their revenge against the stomach, which they planned to starve, but they soon dis-

covered that their plot was destroying the whole body. So they found that the stomach was, after all, working in a very important way. It actually was nourishing them in return for the food so that the blood produced might convey nourishment to all the body."

The people caught the meaning of the parable and realized how necessary each was to the peace of the entire nation. Likewise, the body, emotions, mind, and spirit are inseparably bound together. Whenever a breakdown occurs in one area, it affects the others.

When you smash your finger in the car door, what effect does it have on

*"Well, who <u>made</u> the
magic go out of our marriage—you or me?"*

your mental state? When you receive a phone call at 2:00 AM saying that a close relative has suffered a severe heart attack and has been taken to the hospital, how does your body react? When you knowingly lie to your best friend to cover up something you are ashamed of and then lose your temper in defending yourself, how do you relate to God? How does your body react to this?

An important relationship exists between mental health and physical well-being. The brain, though it is the most important organ of the body, is only one of many. But when other organs are injured or become diseased, the brain suffers too. Likewise when one's mental health is good, the other organs of the body benefit.

The social dimension, which has been the major focus of this book, includes all our relationships with others: spouses, children, in-laws, friends, neighbors, and business associates. Problems with people cause us to suffer mental anguish, which consequently affects our physical and spiritual fitness as well.

Individuals suffering under severe marital problems just before a breakup might find that they are irritable, cross, and irrational. They might suffer from a loss of appetite, overeating, insomnia, tiredness, or a total lack of vitality. It becomes difficult for them to put their mind to a task and complete even the simplest responsibilities throughout the day. At last they visit their physician for medication to cope with the stress they are under. The original breakdown occurred in the social dimension, but it also affected the physical health and mental stability.

But balanced living is more than just feeling physically well. Even when mental alertness is added, the picture remains unbalanced. And when we add social fitness to physical and mental well-being, there still isn't balance. Only when we add spiritual commitment do we have all the components that are essential to the harmonious development of balanced living.

Spirituality constitutes a vital component of balanced living, but we often leave it out of our lives. Love to God and to our fellowman, a clear conscience, and service to others completes the picture, vitalizing all life's activities. This is the formula for balanced living. When life has depth, it will have as a consequence greater breadth and greater length.

Your life, the one that you are living now, is the only one you will ever have. Are you happy with the way you are living it? If you are not using it well, you cannot turn it in for a new one later. Are you making the most of this one life that is yours to live?

Balanced living doesn't come by chance or by wishing for it or by waving a magic wand. It comes as a result of a planned life that progresses in harmony with the development of the physical, mental, social, and spiritual whole.

Further reading you will enjoy...

Mallory, James. *THE KINK AND I.*
Mayhall, Jack. *MARRIAGE TAKES MORE THAN LOVE,* chapters 30-34.
Morgan, Marabel. *TOTAL JOY,* Chapter 8.
Morgan, Marabel. *TOTAL WOMAN,* chapters 8-10.
Peterson, J. Allan. *CONQUERING FAMILY STRESS.*
Wheat, Ed and Gaye. *INTENDED FOR PLEASURE.*

"Life is a lively process of becoming. If you haven't added to your interest during the past year—if you are thinking the same thoughts, relating the same personal experiences, having the same predictable reactions—rigor mortis of the personality has set in."
—General Douglas MacArthur.

Have Fun With Your Mate

T Adams

You've heard the saying, "The family that prays together stays together." Some people think that all it takes to hold a marriage together nowadays is more religion and church attendance. But I have observed that unless the family that prays together, also plays together, the members may still go astray.

While Harry and I make no pretense of knowing all there is to know about marriage, we have learned from our years together that a couple must basically enjoy one another. We have fallen far short of the ideals that hindsight readily offers, but we thank God for the good times that we've had in being able to mix fun with married life.

We have taken stock during our marriage of the Christian homes that have succeeded and those that have failed. Without exception we have found that the most successful marriages have added the warmth of fun, laughter, and enjoyable experiences to life.

Up to now this book has outlined principles that will take genuine self-discipline and willpower to put into practice. The benefits of the efforts expended will outweigh the struggle, but

Chapter at a Glance

I. **Family Playing Is as Important as Family Praying**
   A. A couple must enjoy one another
   B. Fun can be mixed with marriage

II. **Marriage Is Not All Hard Work**
   A. An ideal marriage includes—
      1. enjoying one another
      2. having fun with one another
      3. laughing together
      4. delighting in one another's presence

   B. Include a weekly activity that will enrich married life
   C. Make family worship fun
   D. Engage in fun activities daily

III. **Are You Fun to Live With?**
   A. Next to ministers, comedians have the longest-lasting marriages
   B. Laughter is a good tranquilizer for problems
   C. Make today a happy day—
      1. for yourself
      2. for your mate
      3. for your family

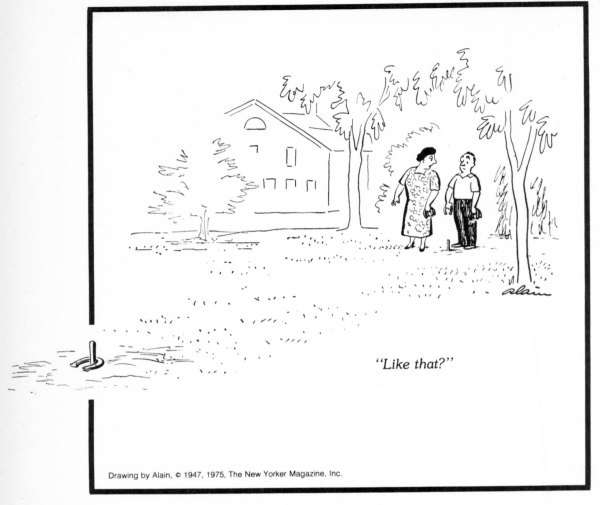

"Like that?"

Drawing by Alain, © 1947, 1975, The New Yorker Magazine, Inc.

nevertheless it takes a lot of hard work to make a happy marriage. But now I want to emphasize that marriage, in my opinion, is not all hard work, effort, and self-discipline. An integral part of the happy marriage is the ability to enjoy one another, to have fun with one another, to laugh and find delight in one another's presence.

From our earliest years of marriage Harry and I have found time, in spite of hectic schedules, to include in each week an activity that will enrich our married life—camping trips, picnics at a favorite spot in the country, dinners out, an evening of games, a hand-in-hand walk beside the crashing surf, a swim, or a drive.

The result? Our marriage—and to God be the glory—grows happier with each passing year.

We have traveled thousands of miles together on a tight budget. We invested in a new pickup truck and an old but roomy and serviceable camper. With this rig we've camped on the deserts of California and Arizona, in the mountains of Canada and Washington, and by the lakes and seashores of a number of states. Some of our most memorable family times have occurred in the fresh breath of nature—a couple enjoying together the magnificent natural beauty that the Lord has provided for His people.

We have tried to interject the aspect of fun into our family worships as well. Instead of solemn occasions where every family member sits stony-faced during the reading of Scripture, we have encouraged creativity. Our worships have resulted in guessing games, twenty questions, pantomimes, musicals, and dramas. Perhaps the most fun of all were the Bible stories acted out by the three children—Carlene directing (because she was the oldest), Rodney obeying willingly (because he was the most adaptable), and Mark dragging his feet (because of his nature). Their reenactments included costumes, scripts, props, and originality.

Harry and I religiously engage in fun activities on a daily basis for our own sake. These activities change with the season and according to the section of the country we live in. But at present they include among other things a morning jog together. This early morning ritual not only provides the exercise we need for better health, but it improves our attitudes, gives us time to communicate, and stimulates a mutual interest. In the cool of the evenings we often bike around the neighborhood or on the new bike path that runs near our home.

Perhaps the most memorable fun activity we engaged in recently was sparked after attending Dr. Howard Hendricks' and J. Allan Peterson's Family Affair seminar. At the close of the meetings, one of the assignments was to think of a creative way to romance one's partner. Harry asked me for a date, and one month later we went to San Francisco with another couple. We lived it up from early morning—

beginning with breakfast out as we traveled. (We *never* eat breakfast out.) We first stopped at Golden Gate Park, where we walked through the botanical gardens. We went on to Seal Rock, where we browsed through shops and toured a fascinating museum of old coin-operated mechanical machines. Oh, yes, we even remembered to look at the seals!

Our next stop was Fort Point, a national historical monument located on the San Francisco Bay directly under the Golden Gate Bridge. Along with our guide, who was costumed in a replica of a Civil War uniform, we explored the soldiers' quarters and gun emplacements, listened to fascinating stories of

Have Fun With Your Mate

List ten activities you enjoy most:

1.   6.

2.   7.

3.   8.

4.   9.

5.   10.

Now list ten activities your mate enjoys most, and share your responses with your mate for insight.

1.   6.

2.   7.

3.   8.

4.   9.

5.   10.

If you are not presently sharing some of them with your mate, which might you enjoy sharing?

1.

2.

3.

List several fun times you have recently shared with your mate that have meant the most to you.

1.

2.

3.

How do you feel?
1. When I share a fun time with my mate, I feel . . .
2. When my mate shares a fun time with me, I feel . . .
3. When I share an activity with my mate that I dislike but my mate enjoys, I feel . . .

past history, and even participated in a mock firing of a cannon.

A trip to San Francisco would not be complete without a visit to Fisherman's Wharf and Cannery Row, and from there we stopped at Ghiradeli Square, where our dates escorted us to the day's finale—a romantic dinner by candlelight at sunset with a view overlooking the bay.

How about you? Are you fun to live with? Have you brought something into the marriage recently that was interesting, challenging, creative, or delightful? When was the last time you did something alone with your mate just for fun? When was the last time you enjoyed a good laugh together?

Did you know that next to ministers, comedians have the longest-lasting marriages? Why? Perhaps because laughter relieves tension. Generally speaking, we don't smile or laugh enough. It's conceded that Richard Nixon lost the election the first time he ran for President because he did not smile enough. During his second Presidential campaign, he was rarely seen in a photo or television interview not smiling. Yes, people respond favorably to smiles and laughter.

Department stores have discovered that their sales go up as much as 20 percent when the clerks smile at the customers. Some companies insist that the executives smile as they walk in the door to begin the day. "A smile sets the tempo for the day," one president explains. "It determines how the employees will feel during the day. It gives them assurance, makes them feel everything is right within the company. If a company executive walks in the front door with a frown on his face, it gives people the impression something is wrong."

Laughter is a way of telling others that you are glad to see them, that things are going well, and that it is good to be alive. There may be serious things to consider, but we'll face them pleasantly together. Start with a smile and take it from there.

Laughter is a wonderful tranquilizer for problems. Charlie Shedd has commented that when a couple learns how to laugh and make merry over mistakes, a wonderful transformation takes place in the home. "High heaven has special clean-up squads," he writes, "which respond to these signals. They come to sweep away the broken pieces and give that marriage a fresh beginning."

A smile is a way of writing your

Now Comes the Fun Part!

Kidnap your wife for a minivacation—an afternoon or evening of something she's been wanting to do. It might include a dinner out at a romantic restaurant. Maybe it's driving through a new housing development or checking out a new dress shop. It could be a drive to the country, a stroll through the park, a visit to a furniture store—anything you know she's been wishing she could do. Secretly make all the arrangements for baby-sitting. Give her only enough warning so she can dress properly. Women love the element of surprise and suspense as well as the change of pace for a few hours.

Create a holiday in honor of your mate. With the children in on the planning, schedule a special day with banners, balloons, a parade through the house, carry-in food, or whatever. Let your imagination go. Make it your mate's special day.

A tour of yesteryear. Spend an hour with your mate in the living room or in the family room reminiscing about the books, family albums, pictures, or furniture there. Remember where they came from, what they mean to you, and the shared dreams they represent.

A late evening walk. Keep your marriage fresh and vital by taking a late evening walk together. Take time to reflect, hold each other close, catch up, and know one another's hearts as you did during courtship.

Reminiscing time. Instead of TV tonight invest an hour after dinner reminiscing with your mate about when you (1) had the most fun; (2) felt the most embarrassed; (3) cried the hardest; (4) were so tired that . . .; (5) never worked harder; (6) felt the closest to God. The family album might help jog your memory. And close your reminiscing time by thanking God for the relationship that you share with one another.

Exploring. Remember that side street or back road you always wondered about? that quaint shop you've never checked out? Your mate would probably love to explore it with you. So set some limits (mileage, time, expense) and let your mate choose where and what he/she would like to explore.

thoughts on your face. It is a way of telling others that they are appreciated, accepted, and liked. And when you begin smiling, you will find others smiling back. It becomes a way of saying, "Thank you. You are making my day more enjoyable. You make me feel noticed, important, and cared for."

There is no other gift whereby you can give so much enjoyment as inexpensively as with a smile. The habit of smiling can be a valuable asset when facing situations that might otherwise cause you to sink in discouragement and despair. As Ella Wheeler Wilcox mentions in her poem "Worthwhile":

'Tis easy enough to be pleasant,
When life flows along like a song:
But the man worthwhile is the one
    who will smile
When everything goes dead wrong.

Make today a happy day for yourself, for your mate, and for your family. Come up with a surprise. Share a funny story. Plan ahead for a special occasion. Attend a class. Go to a new and interesting place or event. Give a gift. Smile.

Laugh. Take time to play. Find a way to have fun with your mate. Make your married life as happy and enjoyable as possible.

Further reading you will enjoy...

Peterson, J. Allan. *THE MARRIAGE AFFAIR*, pages 198-202.
Whiston, Lionel. *ARE YOU FUN TO LIVE WITH?*
Benson, Dan. *THE TOTAL MAN.*
Lee, Mark. *HOW TO SET GOALS AND REALLY REACH THEM.*

"We wouldn't think of building a stone fireplace without stones, or of baking an apple pie without apples. Why, then, are so many people trying to build Christian homes without Christ? They try to maintain 'Christian' principles, establish a 'Christian' home and even use 'Christian' terminology; but without the presence of Christ there cannot be a Christian home. The great and holy God must be living in that home; He must be living in the hearts of those who call that house 'home.'"
—Char J. Crawford

Worship With Your Mate

Although the spiritual dimension in marriage has been alluded to throughout this book, it has not yet been singled out for special attention. But it is, perhaps, the most important part of marital adjustment. The relationship between husband and wife that this book describes is more than a commitment between two persons. Rather it is a three-sided relationship consisting of husband, wife, and God.

Notice on the triangular diagram on page 192, that as husband and wife draw closer to God, they also draw closer to each other! Adding the spiritual dimension, then, transforms the marriage relationship into a powerhouse of strength. Scripture tells, "Except the Lord build the house, they labour in vain that build it" (Psalm 127:1).

If a couple wish to experience complete oneness in marriage they will worship together. Without spiritual oneness there can never be total oneness in understanding, communication, or sex. Spiritual oneness will give you a power beyond what ordinary couples know in their marriages.

Chapter at a Glance

I. **The Missing Dimension**
   A. Human beings are intensely spiritual
   B. The closer spouses draw to God, the closer they come to each other
   C. Complete oneness includes having family worship

II. **The Meaning of Family Worship**
   A. Weekly corporate worship is important
   B. Individual worship is important

III. **How to Worship With Your Mate**
   A. Personal devotions
   B. Prayer
   C. Home worship
   D. Church attendance
      1. "Mixed-faith" marriages have trouble
      2. Four major religious conflicts
   E. Consistency
      1. Religion is a full-time occupation
      2. Allow no double standards

IV. **The Secrets of Success**
   A. Emotions are not the most vital
   B. The use of the will is most important

GOD

HUSBAND

WIFE

Progressive Togetherness

The Meaning of Family Worship

But what does it really mean to worship with your mate? Does it mean that husband and wife regularly attend religious services together? That surely would help, but true worship begins within the quietness of the individual.

Here are five of the most essential ingredients involved in worshiping with your mate:

1. Personal Devotions. The depth of your worship experience is really measured by what happens after you leave congregational worship. What takes place during the rest of the week in your home? At your job? During your social obligations? You are your church or synagogue, and it is your influence in your everyday life that speaks either for or against your God.

There is no way to live a healthy, consistent spiritual life without devoting time to personal devotions. Trying to do otherwise is like trying to drive an automobile without ever filling the gas tank. You won't get anyplace. Your days will likely fall into a chaotic cycle of failure and repentance, failure and repentance, and your restless sleep will mar your nights.

2. Prayer. It is important that you have a private and personal prayer life along with your Bible study and devotions. But how often do you and your mate pray aloud—*together?* Praying aloud to your heavenly Father is one of the best means of improving communication between two people. A marriage can be completely transformed when a couple regularly seek the Lord in prayer together.

You might also notice some additional side benefits from such praying. The other person may remember something important that you have forgotten to pray for. And another interesting thing may happen. Because the sexes are interested in different facets of life, you will be praying for slightly different things. She likely will pray about the marriage relationship, the children, and personal problems. He will more likely pray about financial pressures, his job, and the future. Such praying will likely be on level 1 (see page 78) and will build intimacy. The sharing of common burdens will knit the bonds of love ever more tightly between you.

When a couple learn how to pray together they will have discovered an important preventive measure against marital difficulties. Morning and evening prayer was once an established institution in homes. As the number of prayers in the home decreased, the number of home problems and the rate of divorce increased. The number of couples who go week after week, month after month, without prayer is probably astronomical. According to a survey of marriages taken by Dr. Pitirim Sorokin, of Harvard University, there is only one divorce in 1,015 marriages where Bible study and prayer are

Share Prayer

The concept of "Share prayer" was introduced in the preceding chapter. Respond to the following questions after experimenting with this method of praying together with your mate.

1. How did you feel after first trying this method?

2. What were your later feelings regarding this method after using it for:

   One week?

   Two weeks?

   One month?

3. What benefits have been felt in your relationship as a result of "Share prayer"?

practiced daily.

3. Home Worship. The occasion when father and mother would gather the children around them, sing together, read a story and a verse of Scripure, is just about unheard of in this jet age. I think we may have lost the art of family worship when television came in. Unfortunately, most families don't sense the tragic loss, because they never had such an experience to begin with.

Here, very briefly, are a few broad principles on how to conduct family worships.

(1) Schedule a convenient time that suits all family members. Schedul-

ing can be difficult, particularly as the children become older and the family seems to scatter in all directions—Dad to a committee meeting, Mom to a night-school class, one teen-ager works till eleven o'clock at night and another plays on a baseball team two nights a week. To accommodate to a schedule just about as bad as this in our household, we decided to have family worship first thing in the morning. We all got up a little early, and the kids all came to our bedroom and piled onto our king-sized bed. Worship included a brief Bible passage with an application of the text made so that it addressed our children's needs. A couple of times each week we sat around the fireplace and read stories in the evening, enjoyed music, and planned more enjoyable activities.

(2) Home worship should include music. Children enjoy singing. Even before they can sing they enjoy being sung to. Music creates a worshipful mood and soothes the emotions. For this reason select the songs carefully. Small children like songs with motion and action.

You might allow each child to choose a favorite song. Ask the child to stand up and lead the others in singing it. This not only gives the child a part in the home worship program but it also develops self-confidence. After a few weeks of such a program you will likely find your children happily singing little choruses as they play. How much better this is than to be lisping a catchy beer commercial!

(3) Teach without preaching. During our Compleat Parent Workshops Harry and I introduce the idea of "teaching without preaching." Most parents don't know how to teach without sounding preachy, yet it is so simple! All you need is a set of Uncle Arthur's *Bedtime Stories* (available

194

Spiritual Dialoging

The following completion sentences are designed to increase your intimacy on spiritual subjects. Begin with the easy ones and progress to the more difficult ones. Always begin and end with prayer. Invite God to sit in on one of your spiritual dialogues.

I feel a daily walk with the Lord is important because . . .

I find my greatest security in . . .

In my opinion the ingredients of spiritual living are . . .

My concept of the source of real deep inner peace of mind is . . .

My concept of God is . . .

My concept of sin is . . .

My concept of man's relationship to God is . . .

My concept of how to cope with temptation is . . .

I view death as . . .

If I were enticed into sin, told you the truth about it, and asked your forgiveness, what would your response be?

through the publisher of this book). Let's say that during the week your child has tended to be sassy or forgetful or has fought with a brother or sister. Since the *Bedtime Stories* are indexed by subject, you go to the index, look up a story that deals with the problem, and select a suitable story. Without ever condemning the child's behavior you can teach better character traits.

Bible stories also teach vibrant lessons. If you can tell them in your own words, do so. If you need a little help, Uncle Arthur has also written a ten-volume set of books known as *The Bible Story* (also available through the publisher of this book). The artwork in both sets of books will captivate any child's attention. You might hold a preschooler on your lap while you read, so he can see the pictures. In a few years you can call upon him to read. Involve the children as much as possible in the home worship.

Worships in our home have involved games, charades, and Twenty Questions, as well as discussions of Biblical standards for dating. We've tried to make the topics relevant to our children's needs.

Many parents use felt pictures to tell stories at worship time. Several beautiful but expensive sets are available. When our children were small I purchased pattern books and made my own felt sets out of "pellon" (an interfacing available at your local yardage store). I colored them with crayons and ironed them with wax paper to seal in the color permanently. They weren't as elaborate as professionally made felt sets, but they served the purpose well. Our children had dozens of stories they could tell each other by themselves. I didn't need to worry about their tearing or mutilating the pictures, since they were so inexpensive.

Our daughter, Carlene, has done this in her home. In the family room (where worship is conducted) stacked on bookshelves right at Brian's elbow are neat boxes that contain dozens of story felts, finger puppets, and visual aids. All Brian has to do is reach for them. Carlene has also developed a plan for teaching children under 2. In following this plan the parent repeats the same stories and songs for a week at a time. Very young children learn through repetition. So the same songs and stories are repeated for a week. (For information regarding the Spiritual

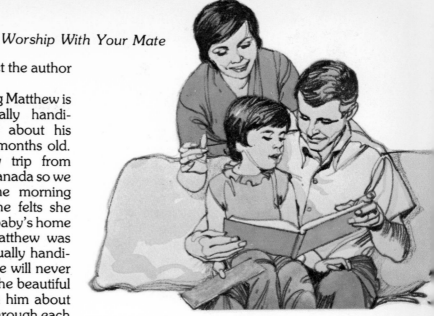

Training Workshops contact the author through the publisher.)

At the time of this writing Matthew is 9 months old and visually handicapped. We first learned about his handicap when he was 3 months old. We made an emergency trip from Fresno, where we live, to Canada so we could see the family. One morning Carlene brought out all the felts she had prepared for her first baby's home worships. Even though Matthew was only 3 months old and visually handicapped (chances are that he will never be able to fully appreciate the beautiful felt sets she made to teach him about Jesus), she faithfully went through each song and activity with him. With my eyes swimming in tears, I couldn't help but ask God "Why?" when so many mothers have normal, healthy babies but are completely unconcerned with the spiritual development of their children.

Each home worship should include something for every child to do. Children (as well as adults) learn by doing. This is why it is important that each child lead a song, wave a rainbow, or place felt pictures on a flannel board.

Keep the worship brief, varied, and informal. If a young child reaches over and pulls your hair it isn't because he is bad or bored. He seeks attention. The attention span of young children is very short.

(4) Talk to God. The entire home worship period should lead toward "talking with God." Build toward this time with eager anticipation. Teach the children to talk to Him as they would with a friend. You may want to try a "conversational prayer" approach with children. You might thank the Lord for something and ask each of the children in turn to give thanks for something. Next you might pray about a certain problem, then allow each of the chil-

dren to pray about a problem. Such a conversational approach will hold the children's attention much longer. It also eliminates some of the impatience as the child waits for others to finish long prayers before he has his turn.

Prayer with children should include thanksgiving for blessings. Also remember sick friends, unsaved relatives, family problems, religious leaders, and missionaries. Make your prayers specific so that the children begin to expect specific answers.

4. *Regular Church Attendance.* Most brides and grooms have a religious rather than a civil wedding ceremony. Why? Is attendance at religious services an important factor in marriage? In what ways does worshiping together affect marriage? What effect does regular church attendance have on a couple, their marriage, and the children born to them?

Researchers have conducted numerous studies on the divorce statistics. All statistical data gathered to date show that those with "mixed-faith" marriages (in other words, those who do not worship together) experience trouble sooner after marriage, seek separations sooner after the wedding,

Spiritual Goals

Someone has said, "Only five percent of the people write out their goals, but of those who do ninty-five percent fulfill them." Someone else has said, "He that aims at nothing always hits it!" In the space provided below, write out your spiritual goals.

1. Where am I in my Christian growth?

2. Where do I want to be in my Christian growth?

3. What will I do personally to reach my goal?

4. What will I do for others (including my church) to reach my goal?

and experience more divorce than do couples who worship together.

Why is the divorce rate higher among couples who do not worship together? Because of the conflict engendered over religious issues. The four major conflicts in order of frequency are:

(1) Conflict over which religion the children will follow. Will the child attend one church or synagogue, both, or neither? Who will take charge of the religious training? Which Bible lessons will be taught the child? Will "grace" be said at each meal? Will family worship be conducted? Will the child be educated in the public school system or through a parochial school?

(2) Conflict over attendance at worship services. If a couple is of the same faith, then religious activities form an important part of their social life. If they do not share this bond there is a tendency for one to compete with the other for loyalty to his or her organization. Each begins to invent excuses for not participating in the religious activities enjoyed by the other. Conflicts result between the more liberal views of one and the more strict views of the other. The stage is now set for major disagreements regarding places of amusement that the more strict partner feels are questionable or downright sinful.

(3) Conflicts over interference from in-laws. Grandparents will be watching and waiting to see that their grandchild is brought up in the "right" religion and may apply pressure to see that this is carried out. Religious gifts, such as books, figurines, or wall hangings may add to the pressures.

(4) Conflict over the number or spacing of children. Couples of differing faiths have fewer children than average, presumably because of the conflicts. Certain religious groups discourage

contraception, and others advise against bringing children into the world during the "last days."

A study by Landis explored who took the reponsibility for the religious training in homes of mixed-faith couples. In more than a third of the cases the mother took all the responsibility. In most of the other cases the child was exposed to both faiths—sometimes by one parent, sometimes by both. In a few cases the child was actually taken to both places of worship in turn. Those who looked back at the mixed-faith marriages of their parents were inclined to feel that generally it had been a serious handicap in their home lives. Another study showed that six out of ten children from mixed-faith homes ended up rejecting all religion.

Studies also indicate that couples not matched in religious background attend religious services less frequently. And the more problems a couple experience, the less likely they are to attend a place of worship regularly. Apparently the embarrassment over their marital problems, as well as decreased willingness to do anything together, keeps them away. Organized

Putting It Into Practice

1. At a family council this week discuss plans for beginning family worship in your home. At that time discuss the following items:

   a. The time of day that best suits all family members involved

   b. The format these worships should have (take into account the age and interests of all family members)

   c. How each family member can participate

   d. What each family member is responsible for

   e. What materials might need to be purchased in order to have proper supplies on hand to conduct worships

2. What benefits can you see that might result in your own life from:

   worshipping with your mate?

   In the life of your mate?

   In the life of your child?

3. What benefits might result in your own life from having personal devotions?

   a. How can you arrange it so you could have this time?

   b. What time fits your schedule best?

   c. What would you enjoy studying?

   d. When will you begin?

religion is supposed to help people in trouble, but often people are too ashamed to face a seemingly judgmental congregation.

Since one of the prime objectives of this book is to help male understand female, and female understand male, I will venture one more observation. A woman usually views attendance at a place of worship as one of her main social contacts outside the home. She looks forward to attending religious services so she can dress up and be seen in the company of her husband and children. She will likely find the service stimulating and relaxing aside from the spiritual aspects, since it is so markedly different from her life during the week.

Women look to organized religion for involvement with women's groups. It offers women leadership roles, which is particularly important for those who do not work outside the home, giving wives an opportunity to contribute and become involved in worthwhile projects or activities other than homemaking.

The majority of men do not look at such things in this manner. A man's time is more structured than that of the average woman. His occupation often demands that he work nights and sometimes weekends. When weekends come he may feel that he should have the right to do as he pleases without religious activities infringing on his time. Or he may feel that the right to relax and do as he pleases on "his day" is the essence of religion itself.

Even when a couple may share the same religious convictions their involvement in religious activities can become a divisive factor. As he involves himself more and more with the building committee and she devotes more time and energy to organizing women's prayer groups, they can each become more interested in doing their own thing for the church or synagogue than in sharing religious activities. Some organizations are overcoming this problem by asking husband *and* wife to lead out *together* in activities. Harry and I co-chair the social committee at our church. In fact, most of the social committee is made up of husband-and-wife teams along with selected singles. This allows couples an opportunity to work together.

5. *Consistency.* Someone asked a businessman, "What's your occupation?"

"I'm a Christian," he replied.

"No, no," the questioner explained. "I mean, what's your job?"

"I'm a Christian."

"You don't understand. I mean, what do you do for a living?"

"My full-time occupation is to be a Christian, but I am a meatpacker to pay expenses."

O that we might approach our spiritual walk with such dedication and consistency! One of Harry's favorite sayings is: "We are consistently inconsistent." How true this is! Consistent religious behavior in the home is a vital key to successful spiritual adjustment. What we are at home is what we really are. What people see in us at a worship service when we are dressed in our finest is only a façade. The house of worship is one place where we almost always put on our best selves. At corporate worship we appear in all our pious glory!

A father and his young son were riding together one day when a police officer pulled them over and gave a traffic ticket. The father fumed all the way home, vowing he would get the ticket "fixed" and get even with that policeman. Later, when he had cooled down, he realized what his example was teaching his son. The next day he the church and then come home and scream and yell, criticize and blame, nag and judge, will find it difficult to accept the double standard.

A Final Word of Encouragement

Maybe you've tried all this before. You have tried to live a consistent life, but you have failed more times than you care to remember. If you are puzzled over the "hows" of religion you are one of many. I too have wondered whether there was a principle involved, a secret that eluded me.

Yes, there is a secret to maintaining a godly life. The secret is simply this: *A consistent spiritual life must be lived through the will, not merely through the emotions.* We are each given the gift of free will at birth. Under no circumstances will God violate this freedom and attempt to force the will. As a Christian, I feel that one of the most attractive paintings of Jesus is the one in which He stands, knocking, outside the closed door of the human heart. Jesus says, ". . . If any man hear my voice, and open the door, I will come in to him and will sup with him, and he with me." But the latch of the door is on the *inside. We* must open that door. *We* must invite Him in.

We must not gauge our religious experience by our feelings. Emotions can be painfully misleading. We must make a commitment to follow God's will for our lives each day even if we don't feel anything. In God's eyes the transaction is finished. He will handle our emotions, and eventually we will feel different. The emotions do follow the bent of the will. It may sound simplistic to think that this is the secret to living a consistent life. But it is the *only* way.

I would like to close with a personal experience. Harry and I consistently

explained to the boy that sometimes adults say things in anger that they really don't mean. He went to court with this ticket and took his son with him. There he pleaded guilty and paid the fine. On the way home he talked with his son about the importance of traffic laws. This boy will have a healthy respect for the law because of this wise father's example.

The youngster whose parents never attend religious services and who make no pretense about being spiritual can understand the parents' behavior. After all, it is consistent with their irreligion. But the young person who sees his parents accept leadership positions in encountered numerous problems in our early married years. We did not have the benefit of premarital counseling. And even though we were not teen-agers, we were young, naive, and unlearned in the disciplines of married life. We had to work out all problems on our own, and they weren't working out very well!

Harry was training for and finally entered the ministry during this period of time when we were "rocking" along. We went to church faithfully, had family worship with the children, read our Bibles, and did all the "good" things Christians are supposed to do. But things continued to get worse.

Had it not been for our faith we could have thrown our marriage away, figuring that what we had together wasn't worth saving, that it might be better for each of us to go his separate way and not torment each other any longer. But the faith in which we had been reared held us and would not let us go. It became a stabilizing factor. Had it not been for our religious experience, when the going got rough we would have scrapped our marriage. But today we are stronger than ever in the Lord's love and in our love for each

For Women Married to Unbelievers

In 1 Peter 3:1-6 is a Biblical description of how women who are married to unbelievers should act. In your words write what it is you believe those verses to mean.

Are there any changes that you need to make in your life so that you do not alienate your husband from spiritual things?

What is a wife's most effective witness to an unbelieving husband?

other.

What lies ahead, then, is up to you. You can stay where you are, or you can look up. You can say, "Lord, I can't" or "Lord, I will." Nothing will happen through your own efforts, but much can happen when you open your life to divine power.

Further reading you will enjoy...

Christenson, Evelyn and Viola Blake.   *WHAT HAPPENS WHEN WOMEN PRAY*

Christenson, Larry.   *THE CHRISTIAN FAMILY.*
Peterson, J Allen.   *FOR MEN ONLY, Chapter 7.*
Peterson, J Allen.   *THE MARRIAGE AFFAIR, Chapter 7.*
Smith, Hannah Whitehall.   *CHRISTIAN'S SECRET OR A HAPPY LIFE.*

I went shopping for a happy ending. I couldn't find one; so I bought a new beginning.

Footnotes

[1] Dobson, James. *What Wives Wish Their Husbands Knew About Women* (Wheaton, Illinois: Tyndale, 1975), p. 118.

[2] Van Pelt, Nancy L. Unpublished Sex Survey was distributed to approximately three hundred currently married Seventh-day Adventists in various locales across the states. The men and women who became subjects were primarily in attendance at family life seminars conducted for members of the church by Harry and Nancy Van Pelt. The respondents varied in age from eighteen to eighty with the majority between the ages of twenty-five to fifty. The length of time married spanned six weeks to fifty-three years.

[3] Levin, Robert J. and Amy Levin, "Sexual Pleasure: The Surprising Preferences of 100,000 Women." *Redbook* (September 1975), p. 54.

[4] Miles, Herbert J. *Sexual Happiness in Marriage* (Grand Rapids: Zondervan, 1967), p. 78.

[5] Hite, Shere. *The Hite Report* (New York: Dell, 1976).

[6] LaHaye, Tim and Beverly. *The Act of Marriage* (Grand Rapids: Zondervan, 1976).

[7] Pietropinto, Anthony and Jacqueline Simenauer, "Beyond the Male Myth." *Ladies' Home Journal* (October 1977).

[8] Deutsch, Ronald M. *The Key to Feminine Response in Marriage* (New York: Random House, 1968), p. 14.

Bibliography

Andelin, Aubrey P. *Man of Steel and Velvet.* Santa Barbara, California: Pacific Press, 1973.

Andelin, Helen B. *Fascinating Womanhood.* Revised Edition. New York: Bantam Books, 1975.

Augsburger, David. *Caring Enough to Confront.* Glendale, California, 1973.

Bach, George R. and Peter Wyden. *The Intimate Enemy.* New York: Avon, 1968.

Beardsley, Lou and Toni Spry. *The Fulfilled Woman.* Irvine, California: Harvest House, 1975.

Bell, Robert R., ed. *Studies in Marriage and the Family.* New York: Thomas Y. Crowell, 1968.

Benson, Dan. *The Total Man.* Wheaton, Illinois: Tyndale House, 1977.

Bird, Joseph W. and Lois F. Bird. *The Freedom of Sexual Love.* Garden City, New York, 1967.

_____. *Marriage Is for Grownups.* Garden City, New York: Doubleday, 1969.

Blood, Robert O. *Marriage.* Second Edition. New York: Free Press, 1969.

Burke, Louis H. *With This Ring.* New York: McGraw-Hill, 1958.

Bowman, Henry A. *Marriage for Moderns.* 6th Edition. New York: McGraw-Hill, 1970.

Brecher, Edward M. *The Sex Researchers.* Boston: Little, Brown and Co., 1969.

Carnegie, Dale. *How to Win Friends and Influence People.* New York: Simon and Schuster, 1936.

Carnegie, Dorothy. *How to Help Your Husband Get Ahead.* New York: Castle Books, 1953.

Christenson, Evelyn and Viola Blake. *What Happens When Women Pray.* Wheaton, Illinois, 1975.

Christenson, Larry. *The Christian Family.* Minneapolis: Bethany Fellowship, 1970.

Clinebell, Howard. *The Intimate Marriage.* New York: Harper and Row, 1970.

Cooper, Darien B. *You Can Be the Wife of a Happy Husband.* Wheaton, Illinois: Victor Books, 1974.

Daniels, Anna K. *It's Never Too Late to Love.*

Deatrick, Mary. *Sexual Maturity for Women.* Santa Ana, California: Vision House, 1976.

Deutsch, Ronald M. *The Key to Feminine Response in Marriage.* New York: Random House, 1968.

Dillow, Linda. *Creative Counterpart.* Nashville: Thomas Nelson Publishers, 1977.

Dobson, James C. *What Wives Wish Their Husbands Knew About Women.* Wheaton, Illinois: Tyndale, 1975.

Freeman, Lucy. *Emotional Maturity in Love and Marriage.* New York: Harper and Brothers, no date.

Gallagher, Chuck. *The Marriage Encounter.* Garden City, New York: Doubleday, 1975.

Gaulke, Earl H. *You Can Have a Family Where Everybody Wins.* St. Louis: Concordia, 1975.

Gordon, Thomas. *Parent Effectiveness Training.* New York: Wyden, 1975.

Grader, Georgia Kline and Benjamin Grader. *Woman's Orgasm.* Indianapolis: Bobbs-Merrill, 1975.

Guernsey, Dennis. *Thoroughly Married.* Waco, Texas: Word Books, 1976.

Hancock, Maxine. *Love, Honor—and Be Free.* Chicago: Moody Press, 1975.

Hardisty, Margaret. *Forever My Love.* Irvine, California: Harvest House, 1975.

Hathorn, Rev. Raban, ed. *Marriage—an Interfaith Guide for All Couples.* New York: Association Press, 1970.

Hauch, Paul A. and Edmund S. Kean. *Marriage and the Memo Method.* Westminster, 1975.

Hite, Shere. *The Hite Report.* New York: Dell, 1976.

Hoole, Daryl V. *The Art of Homemaking.* Salt Lake City: Deseret Book Company, 1967.

Hulme, William E. *Building a Christian Marriage.* Englewood Cliffs, New Jersey: Prentice-Hall, 1965.

Kammeyer, Kenneth C. W. *Confronting the Issues.* Boston: Allyn and Bacon, 1975.

Kaplan, Helen Singer. *The New Sex Therapy.* New York: Brunner Cazel, 1974.

Kilgore, James. *Being a Man in a Woman's World.* Irvine, California: Harvest House, 1975.

Kinsey, Alfred C., Wardell B. Pemroy, Clyde E. Martin. *Sexual Behavior in the Human Male.* Philadelphia: W. B. Saunders, 1948.

LaHaye, Tim and Beverly. *The Act of Marriage.* Grand Rapids: Zondervan, 1976.

———. *Spirit Controlled Temperament.* Wheaton, Illinois: Tyndale.

Landis, Judson T. and Mary G. Landis. *Building a Successful Marriage.* Englewood Cliffs, New Jersey: Prentice-Hall, 1963.

Landis, Paul H. *Making the Most of Marriage.* New York: Appleton-Century-Crofts, 1965.

Landorf, Joyce. *The Fragrance of Beauty.* Wheaton, Illinois: Victor, 1973.

———. *His Stubborn Love.* Grand Rapids: Zondervan, 1971.

———. *Tough and Tender.* Old Tappan, New Jersey: Revell, 1975.

Lees, Hannah. *Help Your Husband Stay Alive.* New York: Appleton-Century-Croft, Inc.

Ligon, Ernest M. and Leona J. Smith. *Let Your Husband Be a Man and Your Wife a Woman.* Union College, Schenectady, New York: 1960.

Lobenz, Norman N. and Clark W. Blackburn. *How to Stay Married.* New York: Cowles Book Co., 1968.

Mace, David R. and Vera. *We Can Have Better Marriages.* Nashville: Abingdon Press, 1972.

Mace, David. *Success in Marriage.* Nashville: Abingdon, no date.

Maltz, Maxwell. *Psycho Cybernetics.* Hollywood, California: Wilshire Book Co., 1968.

Marshall, Catherine. *Beyond Ourselves.* New York: Avon Books, 1974.

Masters, William H. and Virginia E. Johnson. *Human Sexual Response.* Boston: Little, Brown and Co., 1966.

———. *The Pleasure Bond.* Boston: Little, Brown and Co., 1970.

Miles, Herbert J. *Sexual Happiness in Marriage.* Grand Rapids: Zondervan, 1967.

Morgan, Marabel. *The Total Woman.* Old Tappan, New Jersey: Revell, 1973.

———. *Total Joy.* Old Tappan, New Jersey: Revell, 1976.

Mow, Anna B. *The Secret of Married Love.* Grand Rapids: Zondervan, 1967.

Osborne, Cecil. *The Art of Understanding Your Mate.* Grand Rapids: Zondervan, 1970.

———. *The Art of Understanding Yourself.* Grand Rapids: Zondervan, 1967.

Peale, Mrs. Norman Vincent. *The Adventure of Being a Wife.* Greenwich, Connecticut: Fawcett Publications, 1971.

Peterson, J. Allan. *For Men Only.* Wheaton, Illinois: Tyndale, 1973.

———. *The Marriage Affair.* Wheaton, Illinois: Tyndale, 1971.

Peterson, J. Allan and Evelyn R. *For Women Only.* Wheaton, Illinois: Tyndale, 1974.

Popenoe, Paul. *Marriage: Before and After.* New York: Wilfred Funk, 1943.

Powell, John. *The Secret of Staying in Love.* Niles, Illinois: 1974.

Renich, Jill. *To Have and to Hold.* Grand Rapids: Zondervan, 1972.

Reuben, David. *Any Woman Can.* New York: Bantam, 1971.

———. *Everything You Always Wanted to Know About Sex But Were Afraid to Ask.* New York: Bantam, 1970.

Ritz, O. J. *Reflections on Love and Marriage.* Washington, D.C.: Review and Herald, 1965.

Robinson, Marie N. *The Power of Sexual Surrender.* New York: Signet, 1959.

Salz, Victor. *Between Husband and Wife.* New York: Paulist Press, 1972.

Satir, Virginia. *Peoplemaking.* Palo Alto, California: Science and Behavior Books, 1972.

Scanzoni, Letha. *Sex Is a Parent Affair.* Glendale, California: GL Publications, 1973.

Schuller, Robert H. *Self-Love—The Dynamic Force of Success.* New York: Hawthorn, 1969.

Shedd, Charles. *Letters to Karen.* New York: Avon, 1965.

———. *Letters to Phillip.* Revell, 1969.

———. *Talk to Me.* Garden City, New York: Doubleday, 1975.

Sherfey, Mary Jane. *The Nature and Evolution of Female Sexuality.* New York: Vintage Books, 1973.

Spotnitz, Hyman and Lucy Freeman. *The Wandering Husband.* New York: Tower Publications, Inc., 1970.

Small, Dwight Hervey. *After You've Said I Do.* Old Tappan, New Jersey: Fleming H. Revell, 1968.

Smith, Hannah Whitehall. *Christian's Secret of a Happy Life.* Old Tappan, New Jersey, 1968.

Stewart, John, ed. *Bridges Not Walls.* Reading, Massachusetts: Addison-Wesley, 1973.

Tournier, Paul. *To Understand Each Other.* Richmond, Virginia: John Knox Press, 1967.

Trobish, Walter. *Love Yourself.* Downers Grove, Illinois: InterVarsity Press, 1976.

Umphrey, Marjorie. *Getting to Know You.* Irvine, California: Harvest House, 1976.

Van Buren, Abigail. *Dear Abby on Marriage.* New York: McGraw-Hill, 1962.

Vandeman, George E. *Happiness Wall to Wall.* Mountain View, California: Pacific Press, 1968.

Van Pelt, Nancy L. *The Compleat Parent.* Nashville: Southern Publishing Assn., 1976.

Wahlroos, Sven. *Family Communication.* New York: Signet, 1974.

Wheat, Ed. *Intended for Pleasure.* Old Tappan, New Jersey: Fleming H. Revell, 1977.

White, Ellen G. *Happiness Homemade.* Nashville: Southern Publishing Assn., 1971.

Williams, H. Page. *Do Yourself a Favor: Love Your Wife.* Plainfield, New Jersey: Logos, 1973.

Wittschiebe, Charles. *God Invented Sex.* Nashville: Southern Publishing Assn., 1974.

Wright, H. Norman. *Communication: Key to Your Marriage.* Glendale, California: GL Publications, 1974.

Whiston, Lionel A. *Are You Fun to Live With?* Waco, Texas: Word, 1968.

Art and Photo Credits